IN SEARCH OF HIGHER GROUND

Copyright © 2025 by Chris Sonksen

Published by Arrows and Stones

All rights reserved. No portion of this book may be reproduced, stored in a retrieval system, or transmitted in any form or by any means—electronic, mechanical, photocopy, recording, scanning, or other—except for brief quotations in critical reviews or articles, without prior written permission of the author.

For foreign and subsidiary rights, contact the author.

Cover design by: Sara Young
Cover photo by: Brenton Stanley

ISBN: 978-1-960678-94-2   1 2 3 4 5 6 7 8 9 10

Printed in the United States of America

CLIMBING
INSTRUCTIONS
FOR THOSE WHO
WANT TO REACH
THE TOP

IN SEARCH OF HIGHER GROUND

CHRIS SONKSEN

ARROWS & STONES

To my wife, Laura, and my children, Grace and Aidan. Thank you for inspiring me to reach for higher ground and for keeping my feet on solid ground. I love you.

CONTENTS

CHAPTER 1.	WHAT IS HIGHER GROUND?	8
CHAPTER 2.	OVERCOMING THE OBSTACLES THAT KEEP YOU FROM CLIMBING	20
CHAPTER 3.	BUILDING A GROUP OF CLIMBING COMPANIONS	34
CHAPTER 4.	YOUR ATTITUDE WILL ALWAYS DETERMINE YOUR ALTITUDE	50
CHAPTER 5.	STAYING MOTIVATED ON THE MOUNTAIN	66
CHAPTER 6.	DEVELOPING THE HABITS THAT WILL TAKE YOU TO THE TOP	78
CHAPTER 7.	HIGHER GROUND BECOMES SHAKY GROUND WITHOUT THE BALANCE OF SOLID GROUND PART 1	92
CHAPTER 8.	HIGHER GROUND BECOMES SHAKY GROUND WITHOUT THE BALANCE OF SOLID GROUND PART 2	106
CHAPTER 9.	WHEN IT'S SCARY... DON'T LOOK DOWN	118
CHAPTER 10.	YOUR FINAL CLIMBING INSTRUCTIONS	130
ABOUT THE AUTHOR		143
ENDNOTES		144

CHAPTER 1

WHAT IS HIGHER GROUND?

It is anything good and positive that you desire for your life. It may mean financial freedom, early retirement, or the ownership of personal property. It could mean the beginning of a business that, up to this point, has only been a dream. Higher Ground may be the corporate ladder that is waiting for you to climb, the book that is waiting to be written, or the idea that is waiting to become a reality. It could mean a better way of life, a healthier marriage, or successful parenting. It may be freedom from an addiction or overcoming a past hurt that continues to damage your present and, likely, your future. Simply put, Higher Ground is the place where you live out your dreams.

Higher Ground is different for everyone. Its path is different, the obstacles vary, and the surroundings rarely look the same. Although it varies in size, shape, and color, what it takes to get to Higher Ground is often the same. Dreams, goals, taking risks, letting go of fear and insecurity, good character and mental attitude, the right motives, and accountability are all things you must place in your backpack as you journey up the mountain to this place called Higher Ground.

Many years ago, I was invited to go on a long backpacking trip. Those who know me well know that I am not much of an outdoors person. My idea of the outdoors is lying by the pool at the Marriott. To be a part of this backpacking trip, I was told I would have to attend an orientation meeting in which we would receive instructions on what to bring and how to prepare. Against my better judgment, I attended this meeting and received the information. The guide for the trip had divided up the list of who would bring what. Each person was assigned various tasks and duties to help make the trip successful. I purchased twenty-one of my assigned items, and in a few short days, I found myself on a week-long backpacking trip that I will never forget.

We drove all night to the mountain we were to climb, until finally we arrived. With very little sleep, we began to climb the mountain. All we did was climb for the next eight hours. The guide and the few who had been on a trip like this were doing fine. Those of us, including myself, who had never been on a backpacking adventure felt like we were dying. After hours of climbing and complaining, we finally arrived at a site where we unpacked, cleaned up, and ate. Even though it wasn't very comfortable, we slept like babies through the night.

The next morning, however, the guide woke us up and told us it was time to pack up and continue the climb up the mountain! I honestly thought that we had arrived the day before, that our climbing days were behind us. I tried to reason with the guide and asked him the difference between staying where we were and climbing higher. The trees looked the same and the ground looked the same, so how could climbing higher add anything new to our experience? After much pleading, complaining, whining, and anything else I could do to change his mind, we moved on. We continued to climb all day until we arrived at our final destination, just about sunset. I was so tired that after eating and cleaning up, I fell asleep immediately. The next morning, I awoke and realized that we were at the top of the mountain. The guide was absolutely right. The trees looked different, the air was cleaner, and the surroundings were only something I had seen on a postcard. I realized something that morning that I will never forget—that the view is always better at the top of the mountain. Somehow, when you finally arrive at Higher Ground, you forget all the work that it took to get you there!

> **WITHOUT A DREAM LIFE BECOMES SOMETHING TO BE ENDURED, NOT ENJOYED.**

The first characteristic to reaching Higher Ground is found in this story of my mountaintop experience. You see, the difference between me and the guide was that he had been to the top and I had not. He had a picture in his mind of what it looked like, and I had never seen it. The mountain top was a place he loved, a passion he had, a dream that so captured his thoughts, that fatigue would not and could not stand in the way.

You see, that's the power of a dream. It becomes your compass, your passion, your love, your guide and your thoughts. Dreams become a sense of purpose and direction for where your life is headed. Without a dream, life becomes something to be endured—not enjoyed. Life becomes something where we get by but not ahead. And once you get a small taste of arriving at the destination of your dream, you'll never go back.

Jim Marshall has been described as the most indestructible man to ever play professional football. In a sport where thirty is considered old age, he played defensive end until he was forty-two, starting in 282 consecutive games. He is what famous quarterback Fran Tarkenton called, "The most amazing athlete I've ever known in any sport."[1]

Jim, however, has had his share of struggles. He's suffered a gunshot wound, has been sick with pneumonia twice, has been in several automobile accidents, has undergone dramatic surgery, and was once caught in a blizzard, in which all his friends that were with him died. Jim understands what it means to face trials. The secret of Jim's amazing success lies in his two guidelines: find a direction and dedicate yourself to it. And remember, you can go as far as you want to go if you have a dream. Jim has realized the power of a dream, and, more importantly, he has lived it out.

The first step towards Higher Ground is knowing your dream and committing to it. Take a look at the four ways to clarify your dreams and move towards fulfilling them.

DREAM WITHOUT RESERVATION

In other words, don't be afraid to dream! Dream big; it doesn't cost anything, it doesn't hurt you, and it won't damage you emotionally. It won't abandon you, reject you, or do anything harmful to you. Dreams are wonderful! They are a blank page in which to write your deepest thoughts. There is a canvas of potential in which all that is possible is laid out for you to envision.

Often what keeps us from dreaming is the fear of what others may think of our dream. Will they think it's foolish? Will they think I'm out of my mind? Maybe they'll laugh at me when I share my dreams and aspirations for the future!

> **IF YOU DON'T HAVE A FEW PEOPLE LAUGHING AT YOUR DREAMS, IT MAY JUST MEAN YOU'RE NOT DREAMING BIG ENOUGH. —DALE GALLOWAY**

Can you imagine what people thought of the Wright Brothers when they spoke of building a craft that would carry human beings and allow them to soar above the earth? People must have thought it was a crazy idea! People thought that the human body could not handle the speed or the altitude. The critics lined up to take potshots at them. But it wasn't their critics' dream—it was *their* dream. It was birthed inside of them and became a passion in their hearts. The passion grew stronger than the critics, and thankfully, for us, the Wright Brothers dreamed bigger than others thought possible.

The point is that you will have critics, but I have noticed in my life that those who are good at criticizing are rarely good at anything else. Critics are not dreamers; they simply tear down the dreams of others to a level that is comfortable for themselves. Tearing down the dream releases them of the responsibility to live their lives at a higher level. Critics will always be there, but remember, in the end, criticism always discredits the critic. Dale Galloway, in his book *Leading with Vision*, said, "If you don't have a few people laughing at your dreams, it may just mean you're not dreaming big enough."[2] So be a dreamer and dream big!!

PUT YOUR DREAMS IN WRITING

Less than 5 percent of people ever put their dreams and visions for the future onto paper. I don't know what it is about writing your dreams down, but it just seems to help. Dr. Gail Matthews, a psychology professor at the Dominican University in California, found:

> *Seventy-six percent of those who write down their goals, actions and provided weekly progress to a friend successfully achieved their goal. This result is 33 percent higher than those participants with unwritten goals, with a success rate of only 43 percent of goals achieved."*[3]

I believe that. I have seen it work in my life, and I have seen it work in the hundreds of lives that I have personally worked with.

IT HAS BEEN SAID THAT IF YOU DON'T PLAN, THEN YOU ARE PLANNING TO FAIL.

I have one brother who struggled with drug addiction for years. When he finally decided to clean up his life, he came to stay with my wife and me for a while. The first thing I had him do was write out his dreams to paint a picture of how he wanted his life to look three years from now. His list included: a steady job, a wife to love, a checking account (which he had never had), being drug-free, repairing the damage on his teeth that had been done from his substance abuse, and a few others. After he wrote those dreams down, nearly every one of them came true. There is just something simply magical about writing them down.

John Goddard dared to dream. At the young age of fifteen, he made a list of all the things he wanted to do in his life. That list contained 127 goals he hoped to achieve. It included such things as: explore the Nile, climb Mt. Everest, study primitive tribes in the Sudan, run a five-minute mile, read the Bible from cover to cover, dive in a submarine, play "Claire de Lune" on the piano, write a book, read the entire *Encyclopedia Britannica*, and circumnavigate the globe.[4]

It has been reported that John Goddard has reached 103 of his 127 goals. He is still looking forward to visiting all 141 countries in the world (so far, he has visited 113), exploring the entire Yangtze River in China and visiting the moon. John Goddard has experienced more than most people would in five lifetimes. But it all started at age fifteen when he put his dreams to ink.

I challenge you to do that. Put your dreams on paper. Taking dreams and writing them down is the beginning step to charting a course for success. It's taking them out of your head and heart and putting them down on paper that allows your dream to move from emotional to physical, from something you feel to something you can begin to see.

MAKE A PLAN FOR YOUR DREAMS

Not having a plan is probably the biggest mistake people make. It has been said that if you don't plan, then you are planning to fail. I speak to people every week of the year and have the opportunity to meet a variety of individuals. I often hear people tell me of their dreams. They tell me, "I want to be financially free, own a bigger home, start a business, learn an instrument, write a book," and many other dreams that are good and positive. My first question to them is, "How? How do you plan on getting this done?" Quite often, they are unsure of their plan to accomplish their dreams.

When a football team sets out to win a championship, that is a dream; what helps that dream come true is carrying out a plan. When an Olympic hopeful says, "Someday I will stand on the platform with my country's flag waving behind me and gold around my neck," that is a dream. Only a plan will make that dream come true. When a high school graduate fantasizes about receiving a doctorate in his or her choice of study, that is a dream several years away. Unless there is a plan put into place, that student's dream will remain a dream for the rest of his life.

Dreams are a wonderful thing, but the point of a dream is that at some place in your life, that dream will come true. Putting a plan together is what will bring a dream to reality. Dreams are abstract without action, but when you put a plan into motion, the gap between aspiration and reality is bridged. What you need is structure—clear steps and priorities that transform ideas into achievable goals. The beautiful thing about a plan is that once you accomplish one step, your momentum builds as confidence is cultivated. As dreamers, we have to see physical evidence—even if only a little—of our ability to make it happen.

I have several dreams for my life. One of those dreams was to successfully plant a church in Corona, California. So, I sat down and put my dreams to ink, and then I created a plan. It included funding, building a team, mission statements, core values, timelines, and promotional plans. I not only placed on paper what I needed but the steps necessary to see them accomplished. The task of planting a church is a difficult one, but having a plan to follow makes it a whole lot easier. My plans became the blueprints, and all I needed to do was follow the outline.

Let me give you a quick plan on how to put your dreams to work:

1) **Dream Clarification:** What is the dream or goal that you would like to accomplish? Let's use an example and say that you wanted to learn a second language. The first thing you want to do is take a blank piece of paper and write at the top, "Learning a second language."

2) **Assessment:** Where are you now? What are the resources you have to accomplish the goal of a second language? Do you know someone who can teach you? Do you have the finances to pay for instruction? Write the resources down.

3) **Goal Setting:** When do you want to have this accomplished? Write a date on which you will have learned this second language.

4) **Implementation:** How do you plan on getting there? After you have considered your resources and the deadline you have set, you must now lay out a step-by-step plan to accomplish the goal. Try to break it down into a few steps, so you don't get so overwhelmed. Also, put a date next to each step so you can measure whether or not you are on track to accomplish your goal.

5) **Evaluation:** When the deadline arrives, go back to your paper and evaluate whether you hit the goal. If you hit the goal, congratulate yourself. If you came up short, figure out why.

This simple method will work with any dream: starting a business, buying a house, or whatever your goal may be. How you choose to plan out your dreams is up to you, but whatever you do, plan them out. Create a footprint to follow. It was Nelson Algren who once said, "Life is hard by the yard . . . but you don't have to do it by the yard. By the inch it's a cinch."[5]

BE COMMITTED TO DOING WHATEVER IT TAKES

We are a society that is great at starting things. We start diets that we never finish, sign up for gyms we never attend, and make commitments we don't follow through with. Many have made the long walk to the altar to say, "I do" but then "never did." We are a society that follows through with very little. I have learned throughout the years that character is not only made in crisis, but it is also displayed in crisis. That the true character of an individual is not what they start, but what they finish. Anyone can start a marathon, but it takes stamina to finish it. Anyone can set out to swim the English Channel, but it takes endurance to complete it.

Dreams, goals, and plans must be supported by the attitude of the dreamer that says, "I will do whatever it takes to make this happen. It may pull me out of my comfort zone or force me to change, but I will do whatever it takes to make it happen." This attitude must be taken on by those who dare to dream. Consider the discouragement these people must have faced:

» *"You're foolish to try to sell sparkling water in the land of Coca-Cola drinkers"*[6] (a consulting firm's criticism of Gustave Leven and his idea to bring Perrier to the US).
» *"You have a nice voice, but it's nothing special"*[7] (voice teacher about Diana Ross).

- » *"You're fired from this newspaper because of a lack of creativity"*[8] (told to Walt Disney).
- » *"How long will you go on training all day in a gymnasium and living in a dream world?"*[9] (Arnold Schwarzenegger's family's plea for him to get a "respectable" job).
- » *"It's a cutthroat business, and you've got no chance of success"*[10] (accountant for Estée Lauder).

These are just a few people who had to work past criticism, obstacles, hard times, financial hardship, and many other trials that can face a dreamer and cause them to quit. You must set out with the mental attitude that you will make it.

In the 1970s, there was a popular sitcom called *Laverne and Shirley*. This hilarious duo would come into homes all across America making people laugh. One trademark for this show was a little song that they would sing to lift each other's spirits. The song said, "Just what makes that little ant think, he can climb a rubber tree plant, anyone knows an ant, can't, climb a rubber tree plant, but he's got high hopes."[11]

Decide right now that you will be someone who never gives up. You're going to dream, make plans, follow through, and most importantly, you will never ever, ever, ever give up!

CHAPTER 2

OVERCOMING THE OBSTACLES THAT KEEP YOU FROM CLIMBING

Let me take you back for a moment to the backpacking trip I told you about in chapter 1. It was my one and only experience backpacking, and although I am not a camping type of person, I must admit I did enjoy it. The beauty of the mountains, the serenity of the peaceful surroundings, and the enormous trees that towered over us were quite a sight to see. However, the thing that I enjoyed the most was the sense of accomplishment once we had reached the top of the mountain.

As I think back to that week, I remember many times not wanting to climb the mountain. I remember at the original orientation thinking to myself, *Will this really be worth it, all this work?* I thought of backing out before we even began the trip. Then once we started the trip, there were several times when I thought how I would love to stop climbing and turn around and head back down the mountain. Many of us were tired of climbing, and our bodies began to ache. The quality of the food was poor, there were no restroom facilities, no showers, it was hot, and man, did we stink! There were the bugs and snakes that we encountered, and one night we were awakened by a bear that came into our camp. When that happened, I immediately thought to myself, *This would not happen at the Marriott!*

But as I stated earlier, I am glad we continued the climb; that we did not allow certain circumstances to keep us from going to Higher Ground. Although we felt like giving up, we pressed on and reaped the benefits of all our work. I learned a valuable lesson during that week: on the road to the top, there will always be opposition.

Whatever your dream or goal is, whatever road you want to climb, you can be assured there will be opposition. I heard an inspiring story of a ten-year-old girl named Sarah. Sarah was born with a muscle missing in her foot. This unfortunate tragedy required her to wear a brace indefinitely. She arrived home one day from her elementary school and told her dad that she had competed in "Field Day," a day designed with a variety of competitive events for the kids.

Because of her leg support, the father's mind raced as he tried to think of some encouraging words to give to his daughter, thinking that, with her brace, she probably did not do so well in the competitions. But before he could get out a word, the daughter said, "Daddy, I won two of the races!" The dad couldn't believe it. The daughter went on to say, "But Daddy, I had an advantage." The father thought to himself that the teachers must have given her a head start because of her brace. Before he could say anything, the little girl blurted out, "My advantage was that I had to try harder."

That little ten-year-old girl figured out something that thousands of people are still struggling with daily. She knew that she had obstacles and circumstances that made her situation different. But instead of quitting or making excuses for herself, she simply tried harder. Each one of us has our own set of circumstances, obstacles, and oppositions. They stand there like a schoolyard bully, taunting our dreams and keeping us from moving forward. Over the years, I have seen that the most common obstacles to climbing to Higher Ground are:

1) **Fear**

Fear comes in all shapes and sizes. Fear of the unknown, fear of taking a risk, fear of people, and fear of confrontation. There is the fear of failure, of being embarrassed, of making a mistake, and of letting people down. Fear that you are not good enough, don't measure up, and lack the skills and abilities necessary for the task. Fear of being abandoned, rejected, or hurt by those closest to you. Fear of approaching people, speaking publicly, or sharing your thoughts and ideas in fear of what others may think of you.

FEAR COMES IN ALL SHAPES AND SIZES.

I remember my first public speaking experience. I was fourteen years old and was asked to share at a convalescent home. I had prepared all week to share a brief message with these people—I say brief because it was scheduled to last twenty minutes, but I was so scared, it took only about six minutes and I was done. I remember stepping up to the microphone, and boy, was I shaking. In the small crowd was an elderly man wearing a red cap. Throughout my entire presentation, this man kept yelling out, "Hey, sonny, are you from St. Louis?" I had never met the man before, but there he was, yelling at me in the middle of my most fearful moment, "Are you from St. Louis?" After that, I never thought I would make a life of standing up and sharing with audiences of all ages.

Fear is real. Everyone experiences it at some point in their life. We often respond to people who fear something with, "Get over it; just do it; there's nothing to be afraid of; don't worry." These remedies may come in the spirit of love, but let's be honest, they don't really solve the problem, and may even be insensitive. In a moment, I will give you some antidotes to help you with fear, but let's look at the second most common obstacle.

2) **Insecurity**

Insecurity varies from fear in that fear is "what" you feel about certain things, and insecurity is "why" you feel that way. For instance, I may have a fear of failure, but the reason I feel that way is that I am insecure about my abilities. Insecurity robs us of our potential and ties our feet from marching up the mountain of success.

Insecurities are built into our lives over time. The source of our insecurity may come from our upbringing. Growing up with a mom or dad who we could never seem to please; or growing up in a home where encouragement and love were rarely ever shared or expressed. Maybe even abuse or abandonment contributed to the development of our insecurities. It could have been an experience that took place on a playground many years ago, or maybe a coach that verbalized his or her dissatisfaction with you. Possibly, it was a friend who hurt you, a loved one who rejected you, or a spouse who walked away and never came back.

All of these experiences create this enemy of insecurity in our lives that prohibits us from developing into the person we would like to be.

3) Circumstances

Years ago, I had the opportunity to share the stage with motivational speaker Rudy Ruettiger. Rudy is best known for his hit movie *Rudy*,[12] a story about his life. Rudy is an inspiration to millions. As a young man, he had a desire to play football for Notre Dame. However, his circumstances were piled high against him. He didn't have the test scores or the grades to attend. He was shorter than anyone else on the team and, by his own admittance, the least skilled football player. He fought his way through his circumstances one by one.

Regarding his test scores and grades, he went to a neighboring college and worked hard to get his scores up, until he was finally accepted to Notre Dame. In regard to his lack of natural skills and his size, he had to work harder than anyone else. He was a walk-on that served as an extra on the team to help strengthen the scholarship players. He was told he would never get to dress for the game; however, his heart and passion drove his teammates to stand on his behalf, and the coaching staff not only allowed him to dress for the final home game but to actually play in the game.

THE ONLY THING YOU CAN CHANGE ABOUT CIRCUMSTANCES IS HOW YOU APPROACH THEM.

His name goes down in history as a player for the Notre Dame football team, and his story goes down in history as one of the most inspirational stories of our generation.

You see, it is rare to find someone who is both successful and who complains about their circumstances. But it is common to find those individuals who continually blame their circumstances for their lack of success. Although our circumstances may be rough, they are what they are. If you were born into poverty, there is nothing that will change that now. If you were the oldest and had to work to support the family, there is nothing that will change that now. If you are Black, White, woman or man, abused, or taken advantage of, without sounding unconcerned, there is nothing that will change these facts.

Circumstances are what they are. The only thing you can change about circumstances is how you approach them. You can continue to complain, whine, and gripe, but that will not change your circumstances. It will only prevent you from overcoming them. The choice is simple—if you want to reach Higher Ground, you must stop blaming and start fixing the problem.

When it comes to fear, insecurity, or circumstances, they are all real and serve as obstacles that keep you from climbing your mountain. They are dream stealers, and they will continue to rob you of your journey to the top. Let me give you some antidotes that will help you say goodbye to fear and insecurity and eventually, change your circumstances because to change your circumstances, you must first change your thinking and your self-image.

ANTIDOTES TO YOUR FEARS, INSECURITIES, AND CIRCUMSTANCES:

1) Exchange the lies for the truth

The human brain is one of God's most fascinating creations because it serves your life like a bank. Every day of your life, experiences happen to you and these experiences are deposited into your "mind bank." These deposits become what we call our "memory." When something happens to us, we process that event through our memory, and what has already been deposited in our memories will strongly determine how we respond. For instance, if we have been hurt by someone before and reenter a new relationship, we tend to respond to the new person according to the former experience. It is from this "mind bank" experience that we gain our life's fears and insecurities.

The answer is obvious. If you have some bad information in your "mind bank," you have to begin exchanging that false information for the truth. Recently my personal computer developed a virus. This virus negatively affected every application I ran. The answer wasn't to get a new computer. I simply had to replace the bad information with good information.

CONFIDENCE... IT IS A "MUST HAVE" IN YOUR BACKPACK AS YOU JOURNEY UP THE PATH TO HIGHER GROUND.

As I said earlier, our insecurities and fears may come from our upbringing, our experience as a child or youth, a former relationship, or many other possibilities. We may have been told that we were no good or we would not amount to anything. We may have been led to feel that we were not valuable, useful, loveable or acceptable. The only way to deal with these insecurities and fears is to do the following:

- » **Realize that it is a lie**—Anything that tells you that you are not valuable, loveable, or acceptable is a lie. It may have been information given to you by someone you know and maybe even love, but it is still a lie.
- » **Deposit only positive thoughts**—Begin to think differently. Allow your thoughts to dwell on more positive and encouraging things. Try this: when you go to bed, fall asleep thinking wonderful thoughts. Think of and be thankful for your spouse, kids, job, home, health, parents, friends, faith, or any other good thing that makes you feel alive!
- » **Withdraw only positive thoughts**—Now, that is easier said than done! There are experiences in our lives that continue to haunt us. These thoughts become a prison of mental horror. We replay them in our minds over and over again. Instead of reliving the hurtful past, begin to withdraw positive thoughts. When you are daydreaming, driving in the car, or whenever you do most of your thinking, start withdrawing positive thoughts about yourself and your circumstances. When the negative thoughts begin to show their ugly heads, say in your mind, Not today, you'll have to come back another time!

2) Build confidence in yourself

Confidence is the ultimate remedy for overcoming fear, insecurity, and circumstances. It is a "must have" in your backpack as you journey up the path to Higher Ground. Confidence gives you strength when you are tired, courage when faced with opposition, and a second wind when you feel like giving up. It is difficult to find someone who is succeeding in life, fulfilling wonderful dreams, and truly climbing the mountain but lacks confidence. Confidence and success are deeply intertwined and difficult to separate.

I have two children, Grace and Aidan. Even when Aidan was young, he loved to play sports. He was involved in Little League baseball and enjoyed every minute of it. One of our favorite activities as a family was to go to his baseball games and watch him play. I remember one of his best games. He had been catching and throwing very well, and he hit three home runs. Now, at his age, it wasn't too difficult because it didn't matter how far the ball went; it just mattered if it was fair or foul. If it was fair . . . it was going to be a home run. That's how it goes when you are six years old.

Nevertheless, he had a great game. Since that day, I noticed that every time he stepped out on the baseball field, he was more confident than he had been the game before. Every time he went up to bat, he expected to hit a home run. Every time the ball was hit to him, he expected to catch it. His newfound confidence caused him to practice at home more than ever. And the more confident he got, the better he got. Confidence is like a momentum machine. Once it's rolling, it is very difficult to stop. The more you have, the stronger the machine becomes.

Obviously, I am not speaking of being arrogant or overly confident; I am simply speaking of having healthy confidence in yourself and in your abilities and gifts. A newfound healthy confidence will do wonders for you as you pursue your personal dreams and goals, not to mention bless those you interact with and meet on the way to Higher Ground.

Let me give you some practical ideas that will help you build your confidence. These ideas are based on psychological studies that show when a person changes their "physical actions," their "attitude" can actually begin to change, leaving them with renewed confidence. Let me share with you a few ideas:

» **Smile more**—Smiling is excellent medicine for confidence deficiency. If you are lacking confidence, try smiling more. It is very difficult to feel defeated and to have a big smile at the same time. The physical action of smiling will change your attitude! A real and genuine smile will melt away opposition, will give you confidence, and will brighten up the world of those around you. I was recently in a fast-food restaurant where the girl behind the counter looked to be having a difficult day. I was next in line, so I said with a big smile, "Hi, how are you today?" She looked at me as if I were the only one who had smiled at her in weeks. She slowly smiled back and said, "I'm fine." I said to her, "Doesn't it feel good to smile?" She sort of laughed, and in those few minutes I was at the counter, her entire countenance had changed. Why? Because the physical action of a smile changed her perspective and approach to life.

» **Speak up**—Nothing shows a person's lack of confidence more than when they approach you timidly and say with their head looking down, "Hi, how are you?" It sends a signal that this person really doesn't believe in himself or believe in what he is saying. Practice approaching people with confidence, give them a firm handshake and a big smile, and say a little louder than you normally speak, "How are you?" When asked, "How are you?" I have heard that Zig Ziglar allegedly answers, "I'm outstanding, but improving." Take a page out of his book!

» **Make eye contact**—When you fail to make eye contact when communicating with people, you are sending them a signal. You are saying, "I'm afraid to talk to you; I'm not very confident in myself; I feel inferior next to you." The opposite of that is true as well. When you make eye contact, you are saying, "I believe in myself; I believe in what I'm telling you; I'm above board; and I am confident in myself." Making eye contact not only gives you confidence; it wins you confidence too. Try it, even if you don't feel confident quite yet.

» **Embrace life**—Every day, wake up and wrap your arms around life. Embrace the possibilities before you and develop the mindset of a great day. If you think about it, you are already having a great day because you're reading this book, which means you are alive. If you are alive, that means you have countless opportunities. You have the opportunity to love, to give, and to make someone else's day a great one. You can encourage someone today who really needs it; you can start working on your dreams and start making plans for the future. There are so many opportunities staring you right in the face! So embrace them; embrace life! Yesterday ended this morning, which means today is a brand-new day. It is a blank canvas and you are the artist, so begin now—begin to paint your dreams in colors that were made only for you.

These are just a few things you can do to start rebuilding your confidence level—to start feeling better about yourself and your future. Rebuilding your confidence is a great thing because you can start on it immediately. You don't have to wait for anyone or anything!

As you make your decision to search for Higher Ground, you will run into a variety of obstacles ranging from fear to insecurity to overwhelming circumstances. However, if you will choose to exchange the lies for the truth and begin to build up your confidence, it won't matter what you face as you climb the mountain to your dreams. Your momentum will be so strong that any obstacle will seem like a small bump along your personal path to success.

CHAPTER 3

BUILDING A GROUP OF CLIMBING COMPANIONS

I told you earlier that one of the dreams my wife and I had was to plant a successful church. It was in the early part of 1998 that we decided to go forward with that dream. We began to work on all the plans necessary to make this happen. Finances, goals, mission statements, core values, and many other things that are necessary as you take on such a large project. My wife and I realized that in order to climb a mountain this high, we were going to need help. We needed people who would build with us, believe with us, work with us, and become our climbing companions. During the process of preparation, we met with several people and shared our dream and goals for the future. Countless dinners, phone conversations, personal meetings, miles of driving, and sharing with anyone who would listen to the dream. It was an exciting time as we journeyed through the unknown, but probably the most exciting thing to me was sharing with individuals who eventually came on board with us and became a partner in the dream. I knew going into this project that people would be our most precious resource, but I believe I came to appreciate it more than ever.

We built a group of about fifty people who became our partners in this project. Over the next few months, we continued to share the vision with them—about what it meant to be a team, to work together, and to partner with one another. Beyond building a team of people who would assist in accomplishing a goal, these wonderful people became our closest friends. We learned together, laughed together, did social things together, rejoiced with each other, and wept with each other. These people had become, and still are, my closest friends. There isn't anything I would not do for any one of them!

We all realized during that time that if you set out to invest in others, they will, in turn, invest in you. If you sow into someone else's life, they will, in turn, sow into yours. That is the beauty and importance of having quality people in your life.

NEVER UNDERESTIMATE THE NEED FOR PEOPLE IN YOUR LIFE.

You are better because you know them, and they are better because they know you. You help each other excel and soar to places you could never get to on your own.

Whatever your Higher Ground may be—starting a business, advancing a career, financial freedom, or any other dream—your greatest asset and richest experience will always be people. Never underestimate the need for people in your life. I have a friend who runs a very large organization and has multiple people under his supervision. Recently, he told me that he has made a habit of investing in people's lives. Over the past twenty-five years, he has written an average of forty handwritten letters per day. Letters to friends, colleagues, employees, executives, customers, family, and anyone else who came to his mind. I began to think about all the people he had invested in—people he had encouraged when they were down, thanked for a job well done, and congratulated when they had accomplished a task. He has undoubtedly built a large network of people who believe in him because he first believed in them. Simply put—it's not possible to reach your dreams if you insist on doing it alone. More than that, helping others reach their dreams will cultivate a culture of teamwork where *everyone* wins.

With all the investing he has done in people's lives, how long do you think it would take for people to rally around him when a need arose in his life? If he needed financial assistance, wanted to build a team, needed advice, wanted to open a door that seemed to be shut, or needed a favor, he could very easily have hundreds of people by his side ready to help when he asked. Why? Because he has invested in people's lives.

My friend has not made the tragic mistake that many make. First, he has not burned any bridges. In other words, his life has been spent living with integrity and investing in people's lives. People often burn bridges with others and soon they find themselves without a bridge to cross. (We will talk more about how to build bridges a little later in this chapter.) Second, he has not looked at one person and said, "I don't need you," or "You don't matter." He has realized that every person is loaded with potential. When you negatively or positively affect people, you affect not only them but, ultimately, who they influence. Let me give you an example of what I mean.

One time, my wife and I purchased a vehicle from a local dealer in the town where we live. We had been looking for some time, and one Saturday morning, we came across a vehicle that would suit our family. After much discussion, we felt that this vehicle was a good purchase. In less than one month, that vehicle was back at the dealership with problems. It stayed at the dealership for nearly two weeks. Because it was under warranty, we received a loaner car. We were scheduled to spend a few days in the mountains for a special Valentine's getaway. During that trip, we were pulled over by the police because the loaner car had expired tags. Fortunately, the officer let us go, and we were not held responsible. Secondly, while we were in the mountains, it began to rain and snow, and we discovered that the loaner car's windshield wipers did not work. Boy, were we upset!

TAKE CARE OF PEOPLE, AND THEY WILL TAKE CARE OF YOU.

After that trip, our car was ready, but in less than two months, we were back at the dealership again for more problems with our vehicle. After three weeks in the shop, I was a little frustrated and decided I wanted to speak to the manager about obtaining a different vehicle. Over the course of our conversation, I was told that my vehicle was not their responsibility and that they could put me into another vehicle if I gave them additional money. I had never been so rudely treated and felt such a lack of customer care in my life. It goes without saying that we will never buy a vehicle from that dealership again.

In my opinion, the mistake on their side was looking at me as one customer. When I teach at various seminars, I always share with people that every customer has the potential of several more. These people at the dealership must not have realized that I was pastoring a rapidly growing church in the city. I had spoken at every major club function and most of the public schools in Southern California. So, in reality, I was not one customer. I was one customer who, like everyone, had people that they influenced. It goes without saying that when someone asked my opinion of this dealership, I would strongly encourage them to look elsewhere.

That is the power of connecting with people in the right way. Take care of people, and they will take care of you. Your greatest assets and richest rewards will always be your relationships with people. On your road to Higher Ground, it's not stepping on people that will get you there quicker; it's building them up, connecting with their hearts, and genuinely caring and believing that will ultimately help you soar to success. In the top-selling book *See You at the Top,* author Zig Ziglar says, "You'll always have everything you want in life if you'll help enough other people get what they want."[13] How do we connect with people? How do we help them succeed, which in return will always reap a level of success in our lives? How do we build a high level of positive influence on other people? Here are a few suggestions that will help you C.O.N.N.E.C.T. with others.

CARE WITH A GENUINE SPIRIT

The first step in any successful relationship is genuinely caring about the other person—not about what they can do for you or where they can take you, but genuinely caring. Not about how much they can help you or whom they are connected with...but genuinely and truly caring. Caring about the person is more than just a card or a nice phone call; it is truly caring about the person and all they are, all they want to become, their struggles, strengths, hurts, concerns, and everything that makes that person who they are.

This first step in connecting with people is checking your own motives. The intent of your heart must be revealed at this stage. Is the motive for this relationship pure? Is it one-sided? Are you merely "appearing" to care based on what they can do for you, or do you have a genuine spirit that really cares about the individual? This is where you must do some soul searching and figure out the tough question of why. Why do I want to be near this person?

One of the greatest coaches of all time, Green Bay Packers former head coach Vince Lombardi, had a pulse on the importance of genuine care probably more than any other coach who ever lived. Coach Lombardi was quoted as saying:

> *There are a lot of coaches with good ball clubs who know the fundamentals and have plenty of discipline, but still don't win the game. Then you come to the third ingredient: if you're going to play together as a team, you've got to care for one another. You've got to love each other. Each player has to be thinking about the next guy.*[14]

Let love be your motive and genuine caring be your action. It is the first step to a successful and fulfilling relationship.

OTHERS-MINDED

Being others-minded goes against the grain of our society. We are not conditioned to think of others and, most importantly, to put others first. We are born with a selfish desire to think primarily of our own personal gain. To illustrate this, all you have to do is watch a few toddlers play. When one doesn't get his way, he cries, and when the toys are out there, it's everyone for himself. We are all born with this natural, self-centered instinct.

The best way to combat this natural selfishness and to become others-minded is to gain an understanding of the other person's perspective. What are their fears and concerns, and how can I better relate to them? I recently left on a short trip, and when I was saying goodbye to my family, I picked up my son, who was about six years old, and he said to me, "It sure is high up here." I laughed at his little comment as proud parents often do, but then I got to thinking.... he was seeing it from my perspective, which was different from his own.

THE #1 COMPLAINT AMONG EMPLOYEES ACROSS AMERICA IS THAT THEY DON'T FEEL APPRECIATED.

I began to think about the times I walked with him in the mall and said, "Hurry up, son, you're walking too slow." Or the times we took family walks around the block, and he would stop and look at the flowers, grass, sprinklers, ants, or anything else that intrigued him. Or the time my little girl came running to the front door in fear of a little dog that was about the size of her foot. I never once truly considered my children's perspectives. My son's legs were smaller, and his steps were shorter, so he walked slower. The little dog whose chasing and barking made him appear larger and more dangerous than he was induced fear in my daughter. This was their perspective, not mine. It was their fear, not mine. But my job as a parent is to see things from their perspective. This is the only way I can truly connect with them. Other people may have fears and concerns that you do not have. Try to look at it from their perspective, and it will help you connect with them at a higher level. This may involve asking them questions like, "How do you see this?" or "Why do you see it this way?" Express to them that the questions may help you understand their perspective a little better.

NURTURE OTHERS

Nurturing people is the third ingredient of successful relationships. Nurturing them does not mean that they are below you; it simply means that you want to help them grow. Think of it as a garden. A garden is a place where seeds are planted. It must have the best of care and be handled with gentleness and kindness. Its partner, the gardener, must be committed to bringing out all the beauty and color that lies deep within the essence of every seed. Nurturing a garden is a lot like nurturing a successful relationship. It is expressing love, gentleness, and kindness in such a way that it brings out the best in the other person. Let me give you a few examples of ways to nurture your relationships:

> » **VERBALIZE ENCOURAGEMENT**—Learn to be someone who encourages people often. Find reasons to encourage and build up those around you. When you see a job well done, when someone goes the extra mile, let them know that you

recognize it, and verbally express your appreciation and encouragement. Be free and generous with your praise. You will find that people will connect with you quickly and easily when they hear your genuine voice of praise.

» **SEND NOTES OF PRAISE**—Make it a habit to write out at least two to three encouraging notes per day to the people in your life. There is something special about receiving a handwritten note in the mail from someone. It doesn't have to be a long note, just a few sentences telling them how much you appreciate them or recognize them for something they've done. The #1 complaint among employees across America is that they don't feel appreciated. Do something about that. Make the effort every day to value those around you.

» **APPLAUD PUBLICLY**—If you're a leader of any sort, take the opportunity to recognize people publicly. Whatever meetings you host, find time in the agenda to stop and recognize someone for their efforts or success with a certain task. If someone put your meeting room together or put together the packet or presentation, or if there was something good that happened recently, take a moment to honor that person or persons. It will encourage them and inspire them to continue pursuing excellence in their life.

NEVER BREAK TRUST

Trust is something that takes years to gain and moments to lose. Without trust, there is no foundation for a successful relationship. Trust is the glue that holds all relationships together. To connect with people, they must trust you. They must believe your words, respect your actions, and trust your heart. This kind of trust can only be gained through a life lived with integrity. People often make the fatal mistake of minimizing the importance of integrity by showering their relationships with a charming personality. What they don't realize is that your personality may win you friends, but without trust, your friends will never climb with you.

BE SOMEONE WHO HELPS OTHERS WIN, AND, IN THE END, YOU WILL WIN TOO.

Bill Kynes expressed the difficulties of trust when he wrote:
*We thought we could trust the military,
but then came Vietnam;
We thought we could trust politicians,
but then came Watergate;
We thought we could trust the engineers,
but then came the* Challenger *disaster;
We thought we could trust our broker,
but then came Black Monday;
We thought we could trust the preachers,
but then came PTL and Jimmy Swaggart.
So who can I trust?*[15]

In our society, trust is hard to gain. So, live a life that can be trusted. When people can trust you, they will connect with you, climb with you, and ultimately help you reach Higher Ground!

EMPHASIZE THEIR STRENGTHS

Another ingredient in connecting with people is to emphasize their strengths. Help them to see their gifts, abilities, and strong points.

Dr. Robert H. Schuller once wrote, "The truth is that the average 'bottom of the ladder' person is potentially as creative as the top executive who sits in the big office. The problem is that the person on the bottom of the ladder doesn't trust his own brilliance and doesn't, therefore, believe in his own ideas."[16]

Everyone has the potential to do great and wonderful things. They are unique creatures of God who are made for wonderful works. "Connecting" with others means helping them understand and believe in their abilities; it requires helping them realize they are a well of fresh water waiting to be tapped.

Nathaniel Hawthorne was heartbroken when he went home to tell his wife that he had been fired from his job and that he felt like a failure. His wife responded to this new information by saying, "Good, now you can write your book." Obviously unsure of how they could ever survive without a steady stream of income, to his amazement, she opened up a drawer full of money that she had been saving, waiting for the day Hawthorne could tap into the genius she knew he always had.[17] From her confidence in her husband's ability came one of the greatest novels of American literature—*The Scarlet Letter*.[18]

CREATE AVENUES OF SUCCESS

When you think of the familiar saying, "What goes around, comes around," you tend to think of negative actions. If you are dishonest, lie, or cheat, it will come back to haunt you in the end.

But have you ever thought of associating this familiar saying with a positive action? For instance, if I sow seeds of success in other people's lives, then according to this adage I will reap my own success. This is true! If you will help those you are connected with succeed in their lives, you will never lack in your own success.

It is a great passion of mine to see others succeed. Whether it be the church where I pastor or in my personal business, I want to see others succeed. The more I tend to follow this belief of investing in others, the more successful my personal dreams become. It is a personal mission of mine to create avenues of success for the people I work with. I want to help create a path that will successfully lead them to their personal Higher Ground. Listed are two ways to help create avenues of success for others and for yourself:

» **PUT WINS UNDER THEIR BELT**—I have a painting in my office that says, "Nothing succeeds like success." This painting rings true that the best momentum in life is a win! Have you ever watched a professional basketball game where the other team is consecutively scoring, so the opposing team calls a time-out—not just to regroup but to stop the momentum of the other team? Each team realizes the momentum created when the other team is succeeding. A person who truly connects with others helps them to win. They help by setting them up for success. Be someone who helps others win, and, in the end, you will win too!

» **GIVE AWAY THE CREDIT**—Whenever possible, give the credit away. Let it be the other person's idea, the other person's concept, even when you know it was mostly yours. By letting the other person shine, you will give them a confidence they have never felt. Giving away the credit is difficult, especially for those who struggle with insecurity or jealousy. These two emotions will cause you to take the credit rather than give it away. I once read that the mark of a true leader can be noted as follows: "When things go right, they look out the window; when things go wrong, they look in the mirror."[19] If you struggle with this, try to keep in mind what I mentioned earlier—what goes around, comes around. Let others shine, and your personal road to Higher Ground will be lit with success.

TAKE OTHERS WITH YOU ON THE JOURNEY

As you take your personal journey down the road that leads you to all your dreams and goals, your journey will always be more rewarding and enjoyable if you take people with you. Obviously, you cannot take everyone, and quite honestly, many will be unwilling to go. They will be unwilling to pay the price or to sacrifice what is necessary. But embrace those who are willing to climb with you and become part of your journey, and take them along for the ride. Let them partner with you and share in the success. You will never accomplish alone all that can be accomplished together. So, find the eagles that are willing to fly with you and let them fly. Free of selfishness, jealousy, criticism, and insecurities, take your team of eagles with you and fly on the wings of encouragement, compassion, generosity, and love.

"We did not come here to 'compete' with one another, but to 'complete' one another" has been attributed to the famous basketball coach, Pat Riley. If you can, grab hold of the concept that people are your most precious resource and begin to treat them that way. If you can, realize that by helping others succeed, you succeed as well. If you can, get a handle on what it takes to really connect with people. If you can see the value of taking others with you on your journey, then you are ready to fly. You can begin to experience all that you once thought was impossible. You are ready to spread your wings and begin the spectacular search for Higher Ground.

CHAPTER 4

YOUR ATTITUDE WILL ALWAYS DETERMINE YOUR ALTITUDE

Imagine, if you will, that you are at home, comfortably sleeping in bed. It is 2:30 a.m., and your house is filled with a sense of peace and serenity. Suddenly, you are awakened by the loud ringing of your cell phone. You quickly roll over and grope around, feeling for it. Once you find it, answer the call, and place it to your ear, what news do you think you are about to receive? Positive or negative?

Your car is making a funny noise, so you reluctantly take it to your local mechanic. He takes a quick look at the car and lets you know that further diagnosis will be necessary. You leave the car at the shop and go about your day. A few hours go by, and you receive a call from the mechanic. As he begins to tell you what's wrong with the car, what kind of thoughts are you having? Positive or negative?

Your boss tells you that he or she would like to see you in their office first thing tomorrow morning. You say yes as if you have an option, and you head home for the evening. Your boss rarely talks to you, so your mind begins to wrestle with what the subject will center around. You quickly evaluate your progress at work. Your mind gives you an account of your last few days and over and over, you begin to reevaluate things you may have said, projects that were due, or anything else that would help you solve the mystery of your boss's request. After a long night of tossing and turning, you get up, get ready, and head for work. When you arrive, you go straight to your boss's office and sit as *confident*ly as possible in front of his or her desk. Now tell me, what is going through your mind . . . positive thoughts or negative thoughts?

> **A POSITIVE ATTITUDE BECOMES THE FUEL TO IGNITE YOUR SPIRIT AS YOU SET YOUR COURSE FOR SUCCESS.**

In each of these scenarios, there is a good chance that you were quicker to think in the negative rather than the positive. Unfortunately, we as people tend to lean toward a negative mental outlook. A variety of reasons cause us to believe the best for the next guy but not for ourselves. It's like Murphy's Law: "If it can go wrong, it will." Most people think that for themselves! They feel that opportunities and good fortune happen to others but are not reserved for them. Have you ever been in a grocery store and looked at two checkout lines and had to make a decision about which one you would go to? Then you catch yourself thinking, *It doesn't matter which one I choose; the line I choose will be the slowest one.* We take this kind of negative, pessimistic approach, and we try to carry it with us on the road to Higher Ground, but it doesn't work. Negative thinking will prohibit you from reaching your fullest potential and will weigh you down until you don't want to climb anymore.

The good news is that if a negative attitude is "death" to a person who wants to climb to the top, then a positive and healthy attitude can be "life" to that same person. A positive attitude becomes the fuel to ignite your spirit as you set your course for success. It becomes a compass that guides you on your journey and leads you to higher places. Nothing can exchange the power and potential that is found when one person goes deep inside their soul and discovers the amazing strength that is found in belief.

- » The belief in themselves and in their personal potential,
- » The belief that anything is possible,
- » The belief that if they set their mind to it, they can accomplish something extraordinary,
- » The belief that greatness, success, and achievement are not reserved for the few but are possible for anyone, and
- » The belief that the Creator has not selected only a handful of achievers but that in God's infinite wisdom, He placed in the spirit of every man the ability to win and to win big!

If a positive attitude is such a powerful tool, then how do we get it? What steps can we take to exchange a negative attitude for a positive, healthy attitude? Before we begin looking at how to change our attitude, we need to stop and look at where our attitude originates. To discover what elements in our lives have given us our current mental attitude, let me give you the basic foundation on which our attitudes are built.

UPBRINGING

Child specialists will agree that your childhood is strongly related to your overall attitude in life. How you were raised, methods of discipline, morals that were taught, and ethics that were modeled all play a part in developing who you've become. When it comes to the development of our attitude, positive or negative surroundings as a child strongly dictate our future mental attitude. Was the overall atmosphere in your home positive or negative? Were the words spoken around the living room or the kitchen table positive or negative? Was your home a place of encouragement or discouragement? Was it a place of image making or image breaking? Was it filled with joy, expectation of good things, and a positive outlook, or was it filled with a doomsday mentality that nothing ever goes right, and the best way to solve problems is to complain about them?

Chances are, if you were raised in a home where you believed the best about each other, your outlook on life was positive and healthy, and instead of complaining about a problem, you figured out a positive solution, then you are most likely a positive person. However, if you were raised in a home where you didn't encourage each other, where the perception of life was relatively negative, and where you found complaining and griping as a part of daily conversation, then you are more likely to have a negative attitude.

In my early twenties, I took up the wonderful, yet sometimes frustrating, game of golf. I never had a lesson; I just sort of picked it up and played with different friends. I wasn't very good at the game, but I enjoyed playing. After a while, though, I really wanted to improve my game. I noticed that I had a problem slicing the ball off the tee. Sometimes, I would play well, but most of the time, it was a disaster. I decided it was time to take lessons. I signed up at a local driving range and expected the instructor to be my saving grace. After about four to five lessons, the instructor finally told me, "I don't know what's wrong. I've never had a student that I couldn't improve immediately." In essence, he was saying, *Your problem is too big, and I can't help you.*

SELF-IMAGE COMES FROM WHAT YOU THINK THE MOST IMPORTANT PERSON IN YOUR LIFE THINKS ABOUT YOU.

Naturally, I felt a little let down, but I still enjoyed the game and continued to play. About ten days passed before he called me at my office and asked, "Chris, did you ever break your arm?"

I was unsure why he asked that question, but I answered, "Yes, I broke my left arm severely when I was about five years old."

He asked me to meet him at the driving range that night, so I did. He told me he was reading a book on golf, and there was a story about a man who had broken his arm as a child. Because of the accident, one arm was much weaker than the other. The instructor told me to split my grip. I did, and the positive results were immediate.

You see, my problem was that my broken arm had weakened me, so I had to change my grip. Many people have been weakened by a very negative childhood, and now it's time to change their grip. They need to do whatever is necessary to change their outlook, to view life differently, to see things in a more positive and healthy way, and to see themselves as capable and full of potential. My golf game needed an instructor to correct it—maybe you will need an instructor (counselor) to help correct any problem you might have. But do whatever is necessary to gain a stronger and healthier attitude. It will become your source of strength in your quest to reach the top.

OTHER PEOPLE

Another part of the construction of our attitude is other people in our lives. People outside of our parents/guardians have a high level of influence and can drastically alter our attitude. They alter our attitude by how they treat us, what they share with us, how they make us feel, and whether we are accepted or rejected by them. If they make us feel positive about ourselves, then our attitude tends to be positive. If they make us feel negative, then our attitude tends to be negative. Psychologist Charles Cooley discovered that self-image comes from what you think others think about you, particularly those closest to you.[20] Throughout your life, different people become very important to you, and how you feel they view you is the basis for your self-image. So, if we have negative experiences from other people in our lives, then our attitude toward life will tend to be negative.

Other people can include:
- » a coach
- » a close friend
- » a teacher
- » a boyfriend
- » a girlfriend
- » a high school sweetheart
- » a boss
- » a coworker
- » a variety of people

The main thing is that we all know someone who, at some point, has had a place of influence in our lives.

Picture in your mind a floor full of children's building blocks. The child puts one piece on top of the other and builds an imaginary building. People in your life are construction workers in your building. They come along and add a piece to your building and assist in creating who you have become.

A little parable titled "The Man Who Sold Hot Dogs" evidently dates back to the 1930s, but it bears repeating today. The story went something like this:

There was a man who lived by the side of the road and sold hot dogs. He was hard of hearing, so he had no radio. He had trouble with his eyes, so he read no newspapers. But he sold good hot dogs. . . .He stood by the side of the road and cried: "Buy a hot dog, mister?". . . and people bought. He increased his meat and bun orders. He bought a bigger stove to take care of his trade. He finally got his son home from college to help him out. But then something happened.

His son said, "Father, haven't you been listening to the radio? Haven't you been reading the newspapers? There's a big recession. The European situation is terrible. The domestic situation is worse." Whereupon the father thought, Well, my son's been to college, he reads the newspapers, and he listens to the radio. He ought to know. So the father cut down his meat and bun orders, took down his advertising signs and no longer bothered to stand out on the highway selling hot dogs. And his hot dog sales fell almost overnight. "You're right, son," the old man said to his boy. "We're certainly in the middle of a great recession."[21]

The point is obvious. The father didn't know there was a great depression. His attitude was exactly the opposite of his son's. Business was great, his attitude was positive, and life couldn't have been better. His daily activities were untouched by bad news because he didn't have access to it. But someone comes along who has an important place in his life, says a few words, and now the father's attitude changes. Not only that, but the father heeded his son's warning, and the outcome appeared to reinforce what appeared to be true. In other words, lies drove a decision that will now adversely impact the father's quality of life, and the reality of his new life will surely feed the lies even further.

People have a place in building your attitude! It's up to you whether you want to add the building block they bring to your life or dismiss it. It's up to you to separate the truth from the lies, what is right and what is wrong. A rule of thumb is this: if what people say or do to you doesn't build you up, challenge you to be better, and come in the spirit of love, then maybe it's not worth adding to the construction of your attitude.

SURROUNDINGS

It seems that most people, if they are not careful, can find themselves submitting to the power of pessimism. This really isn't that hard to do when you consider the surroundings most of us face each day in our lives. A few years back, I was sitting in a hotel room watching TV. During the commercial break came an advertisement of the news that was coming up in the next hour. The broadcaster said, "Coming up next on the 11:00 p.m. news, three people are dead in a high-speed accident, stock prices are threatening a possible recession, and researchers are saying that your drinking water may be connected to cancer." Now, with news like that, it isn't too difficult to get trapped in the web of negativity.

> **THINK YOU CAN, THINK YOU CAN'T; EITHER WAY YOU ARE RIGHT.**

From the news we watch to the gossip we hear, from the constant complaining of those around us to the traffic we sit in, there is a constant war against positive and healthy attitudes. Pressures, problems, and people continue to chip away at our attitude, leaving our mental perception struggling to stay positive. But the fact remains: if you are going to reach for Higher Ground, you cannot leave the power of attitude at the bottom of the mountain. Your attitude determines if you are on the way out or on the way up. Walter D. Wintle said it best:

> *If you think you are beaten, you are;*
> *If you think you dare not, you don't;*
> *If you like to win, but think you can't,*
> *it is almost certain you won't. . . .*
> *Life battles don't always go*
> *to the faster or stronger man,*
> *But soon or late the man who wins*
> *is the man who thinks he can.*[22]

We now understand how important a positive attitude is on your journey to Higher Ground. But how do we get it? What steps can we take to both improve and grow our positive attitudes? Let me give you a few practical steps that will help you obtain the kind of attitude that will keep you soaring to the top.

ELIMINATE NEGATIVE SELF-TALK

Your first and foremost lesson in gaining new optimism is eliminating negative self-talk. Author and motivational speaker Keith D. Harrell once said, "The loudest voice we hear is our own."[23] There are many voices we hear, but the one inside our mind is the strongest voice in our lives. It helps to chart our course in either optimistic thinking or pessimistic thinking.

We are all guilty at times of hosting a variety of negative self—statements. See if you can identify with any of these:

- » I am too old to do anything else in my life.
- » I am not smart enough to do this.
- » I just know it won't work out.
- » I just don't have the time or energy.
- » I'm not as good or capable as the next person.
- » If it can go wrong, it will.
- » It probably won't happen.
- » I just can't do it.

Is there any statement that you can add to this list? What is the one thing you find yourself saying over and over again in your mind? Whatever the statement is, if it doesn't encourage you or bring out the best in you, it's time to eliminate it from your mind. Choosing to be more positive than negative reminds me of a story I once heard.

A man walking through the local park stopped to observe a Little League baseball game. He looked up at the scoreboard to see how the game was going. He saw that the score was 15-0. He decided to walk over to the dugout of the losing team. They were out in the field, but there were a few of them sitting on the bench. He asked one of the boys, "How are things going?"

The little boy, with a big smile, said, "Great."

The man said, "You seem fairly positive even though your team is losing 15-0."

The little boy, without missing a beat, said, "Of course, I'm positive; we haven't been up yet."

Now, there's a little boy who has the right perspective. He hasn't fallen into the snare of negative talk. He believes the best about himself and those around him. He reminds me of something I read recently that simply said, "Whether you think you can, or you think you can't–you're right."[24] Learn to eliminate the heavy burden of self-talk, and it will free you to climb even quicker on your journey to Higher Ground.

MAKE A CONSCIOUS CHOICE TO RISE ABOVE YOUR CIRCUMSTANCES

As I mentioned earlier, Higher Ground for me was starting a church in the city of Corona, California. Though it has been the most exciting adventure I have ever taken, it has not been without a few bumps in the road. There have been a few things that have taken place on my journey to Higher Ground that have weighed me down at times.

I remember it was just a few days before the "Grand Opening" of this church. We had sent out thousands of promotional videos and brochures inviting the community to join us. The outstanding team of people whom I was privileged to work with was ready.

We had done all we could and were expecting and believing for great things. We had signed a lease to use a small facility as our place to hold services. Just about a week before our first public service, I received a phone call from the city informing us that we were not allowed to use our rented facility for church services. I immediately headed down to their offices to discuss the matter. I pleaded my case and literally begged them to reconsider. I told them we had spent thousands of dollars, and all the promotional materials included the address of this facility. After much pleading and a little begging, they told me they would reconsider and let me know.

IF YOU WANT TO SOAR LIKE AN EAGLE, THEN YOU HAVE TO BE CAREFUL NOT TO WALK WITH THE TURKEYS.

As the leader of this adventure, I had to be positive. I had to "choose" and make a conscious decision that my attitude was going to be positive. Was it easy? NO! Did I feel positive? Not really. But I had to make a choice to believe the best, and I wasn't about to let this one issue block my path to Higher Ground. My mind reflected back to the words of Winston Churchill, "I am an optimist. It does not seem too much use being anything else."[25] By the end of the day, I received permission from the city. I later found out that in normal circumstances, it could take up to two weeks to receive permission to use the facility, but in our case, it took a day. Throughout the short history of this church, a few circumstances could have gotten the best of us. But we chose each time not to let circumstances control our destiny or overpower our thinking. I believe optimism is best described in this way:

> *Real optimism is aware of problems, but recognizes the solutions; knows about difficulties, but believes they can be overcome; sees the negatives, but accentuates the positives; is exposed to the worst, but expects the best; has reason to complain, but chooses to smile.*[26]

You see, being an optimist is a choice. You make a conscious choice to be positive no matter what circumstances you face. You can be negative . . . but what good could possibly come out of it? On your personal path to Higher Ground there will always be bumps in the road. Things may not always go right or go your way, but you must choose to stay positive through it all. As I've said before, "You can be happy and stuck in traffic or be mad and stuck in traffic, but either way you are stuck in traffic." So, no matter what circumstance you face, always choose the powerful tool of optimism.

ASSOCIATE WITH POSITIVE PEOPLE

You have heard the statement before, "Birds of a feather flock together." If you want to be positive and remain positive, you must choose to associate with positive people. It is nearly impossible to find two people associating with each other where one is highly positive and one is highly negative. Positive people don't want to always hear how bad things are. They want to embrace life in a big way, and they choose to see opportunity wherever they look.

Throughout your life, you may have been raised in negative surroundings. Your upbringing may have been with individuals who had a knack for finding the worst in every situation. But if you're an adult, now, you get to choose who you associate with. It is your choice to allow certain people into your circle of influence. I have hundreds of acquaintances and multiple friends, but I have only a few people who I allow into what I call my "circle of influence." The "circle of influence" is not necessarily who I influence but whom I allow to influence me. These people are positive, they believe in the best, they see opportunities, not obstacles, they want the best for my life, they add value to me, and they want me to succeed. They are not complainers or whiners. They don't gossip, and a critical spirit has not trapped them. In my eyes, these people are eagles, they are "10s," and I love to associate with them. But keep in mind: it's my choice to allow these people into my "circle of influence," just as it is your choice to allow positive thinkers or negative thinkers into yours.

When Henry Ford wanted to get unbreakable glass for his cars, he wouldn't see any of the experts. They knew too many reasons why it couldn't be done. He said, "Bring me the eager young person who doesn't know the reasons why unbreakable glass cannot be made."[27] The result? He got his unbreakable glass. Henry Ford didn't want to associate with those individuals who didn't see a way. He wanted to be around those who believed it was possible.

Think about the people who are closest to you right now. Not your family members but work associates, social friends, etc. Are these people positive, and do they seem to always find the best in every circumstance? If the answer is no, then the first place you need to look at is yourself. Remember that you always attract what you are, not necessarily what you want. If the people around you tend to be more negative than positive, or if they fail to bring out the best in you, there is a good chance that you have attracted what you are. That should be a warning sign that you need to start the changing process to a more positive way of life. If you want to be a "10," associate with "10s." If you want to soar like an eagle, then you have to be careful not to walk with the turkeys because the principle of association never fails: you become like those who are closest to you.

My final thought for you on this issue of "Attitude" is something I learned while attending a conference with Zig Ziglar. He said, "Wake up every morning and say out loud, 'today is going to be the best day of my life.'" This may seem a little uncomfortable at first, but after a while, you will begin to discover what I have discovered—that it works. That waking up each morning and starting off with the right positive, mental attitude will make a big difference in your life. Begin to observe why life is so great and think about the positive things in your life right now. The people you love and how fortunate you are to have them in your life. That you live in a country of freedom and opportunity. That you may have a car to drive, a home to live in, clothes to wear, and food to eat. That although life may not be perfect, you are better off than the one-third of the world who will go to bed hungry tonight. As you drive home from work, think about the job you have and the pay you earned, and be thankful. Then, when your head hits the pillow in the safety of your home, and you were fortunate to live another day in this magnificent world, you will wake up again tomorrow and say out loud, "Today is going to be the best day of my life."

CHAPTER 5

STAYING MOTIVATED ON THE MOUNTAIN

As you search for Higher Ground in your life, there will be times when you feel like giving up. Times when you feel like it's pointless and you just don't want to try anymore. You'll feel like it's too hard to keep climbing, and you'll simply want to quit. The question is not whether you are going to feel like this at various times in your life. The real question is: how will you respond to those feelings? Will you stay motivated enough to climb the mountain and finish the journey, or will you find yourself lacking the motivation to continue upward?

I'm reminded of a story my friend told me about a young boy whom the schoolyard bully was picking on every day. Each day, this bully would steal this young boy's lunch money, and the little boy was tired of being picked on. One day, on his way home from school, he noticed a sign advertising free karate lessons. He inquired within and began taking his lessons immediately. After about a week of taking lessons, the instructor informed him that the free lessons were only good for a week and that each lesson would now cost five dollars per session. The little boy didn't have the money, and he figured it would be harder to come up with the money for the lessons than it would be to pay the schoolyard bully, so he quit.

The moral of the story is obvious. This little boy lacked the motivation and found it easier to take the path of least resistance. Unfortunately, many people do that. They start off with great intentions but lose their motivation. "I'm going to start a new business, change careers, improve my relationships, establish a stronger faith, develop a non-profit organization, or make a dream become reality." Maybe you've said this or something like this; maybe you have even started taking some steps toward these objectives. But in the case of thousands of people, their good intentions weren't good enough.

Before I share with you "how" to get motivated and stay motivated, let me share with you some incredible benefits of being a person of motivation:

- » **ENERGY**—People who are motivated tend to have a higher level of energy. It's almost as if they don't need as much sleep. It's not that they are running on pure adrenaline; they simply seem to have a higher level of energy than those who lack motivation.
- » **RECOGNITION**—People who are motivated stand out. They are recognized for their motivation and their desire to embrace life and all it has. People admire them, and they find others willing to assist them in reaching their goals.
- » **OPTIMISM**—Motivated people are optimistic. Their outlook on life tends to be filled with optimism. They see opportunities around them, they encourage those they come in contact with, and they add value to people and situations. Motivated people are less likely to allow negativity to have a place in their lives.
- » **ACHIEVEMENTS**—Highly motivated people usually achieve more. They go after tasks with greater zeal and accomplish more on a day-by-day basis. They attack their goals and to-do lists with greater ambition than those lacking motivation.

- » **HEALTH**—Those who are motivated are more likely to be healthy because they realize the value of fitness. They have noticed the difference in their level of energy when they make health a priority, so because they are motivated to be better, they are motivated to feel better.
- » **STABILITY**—Motivated people are more likely to be stable in their everyday lives. This is because they are more focused and know how to stick to the job. They do not waver whenever the ground beneath them begins to shake. They have learned how to stay strong and focused regardless of the size of the storm.

These are just a few of the incredible benefits reserved for those who choose to make motivation a part of their life. The reality is that "motivation" is an absolute must if you desire to reach Higher Ground. However, if you think about it, everyone is motivated by something different. What motivates you may not motivate the next person. Some are motivated by money; that is, they live and work to obtain more money. Others are motivated by recognition. They desire to be recognized and will do what it takes to obtain it. Still, others are motivated by service—they have a passion for helping people, and that is their simple and pure motive.

We are all motivated by different things. Our unique spirits are filled with a variety of passions, strengths, dreams, desires, and motivating factors. What excites your life and makes you tick will not do it for the next person. These motivating factors are what will determine your behavior. Your actions will be a direct result of what motivates your heart.

My wife and I are perfect examples of two people who are motivated in different areas. Over the years, I have realized the lesson I am now trying to share—that we are all motivated differently. Recently, we were discussing our personal desires for our lives. My wife shared that one of the most important events that could happen in her life would be to raise our two children in a loving home with a solid and active faith in God. Among other motivations, her desire for our children is a high priority, and she is motivated by this goal. I share this goal with her, but now, more than ever, I realize that we share different passions and desires. Speaking, writing books, and helping to resource people for success motivates me. But she does not share these same passions. We are unique creatures of God, and He has wired us each very differently.

FIND WHAT MOTIVATES YOU

Everyone has some type of motivation. They have a passion in their hearts that drives them. When you think of someone like Walt Disney, you think of someone with a desire to make children happy and allow adults to feel like kids again. This desire kept him motivated to press on through all the obstacles when others would have quit. When you think of Bill Gates and his desire to see a PC in the home of every person in America, this desire became his motivation and his means for success. When you think of Hewlett-Packard as a company two college kids started in a garage to create life-changing inventions, you begin to realize that each motivation is different and unique. You also realize that these pioneers took their motivation and turned it into success.

Find your motivation. Find the thing that thrills your heart more than anything else, and you will find it easier to sustain motivation doing the thing you enjoy than something you dislike.

You will notice that you don't burn out on your strengths, but you burn out on your weaknesses.

> **YOUR MOTIVES WILL REVEAL YOUR CHARACTER, AND YOUR CHARACTER IS THE PREMISE ON WHICH ALL TRUE SUCCESS IS BUILT.**

CHECK YOUR MOTIVES

The question you always want to ask yourself when it comes to your personal motivations or your Higher Ground is, *Why?* Why do I want this thing for my life? What is my motivation for obtaining this Higher Ground? You might say, "I want to be rich." Okay, then ask yourself, *Why?* "I want to be famous." Alright, then ask yourself, *Why?* "I want to have my own business." That's a great ambition to have, but you still need to ask yourself, *Why?* Your motives will reveal your character, and your character is the premise on which all true success is built. The last thing you want is to build your Higher Ground on a foundation of selfishness, greed, or pride.

In *Speaker's Library of Business,* Joe Griffith writes about the infamous Wall Street arbitrageur Ivan Boesky. He writes that Mr. Boesky was widely known for making money and advocating his belief in business greed. His greed led him to commit a criminal act which resulted in jail time, fines, and a ban on practicing business. Joe Griffith writes, "Amassing money or goods for your own sake may reward in the short term, but over the long haul it destroys those companies and individuals who give in to it."[28] His motivation was making money, but his "motive" was greed. Lesson: always check your motive for whatever it is you want. Keep it free from greed, pride, or selfishness!

Now that you realize the benefits of finding your motivation and keeping your motives in check, let me share some practical ideas to keep you motivated on your journey to Higher Ground.

STAYING MOTIVATED

Stay motivated by viewing your climb one step at a time. Let me take you back for a moment to the backpacking trip I discussed earlier.

When we arrived at the mountain, I looked up to the top as a beginning climber and said to myself, *There is no way that I can climb that mountain. It's too high and too hard. I simply cannot climb it.* Well, as I told you earlier, we did. We struggled, got tired, and felt like quitting at times, but we climbed it. We made it to the top of the mountain, and you know where it all started—at the bottom of the mountain where we decided to take our first step. You will find your mountain easier to climb when you do it one step at a time. If you look at the entire mountain, it will overwhelm you, but if you look at it in bite-size pieces, it's easier to swallow.

In my quest to plant a church, many things needed to be done, and, quite frankly, the entire picture was overwhelming—a team to build, money to raise, facilities to secure, equipment to buy, promotional materials to design, leaders to grow, and somehow we had to accomplish this without any money or people. This was a giant mountain and could have easily consumed me and led me to give up. The answer was to break the mountain down one step at a time. You see, the ultimate goal was the finish line, but taking it one step at a time was the best way to reach the finish line. If you can learn to break down your Higher Ground goals into one step at a time, you will find it a little easier to stay motivated.

Stay Motivated Through Personal Growth

According to recent research, only 8 percent of people who set out to implement something into their lives ever do it.[29] The reason 92 percent of people never finish the task is that they simply lack the resources to stay motivated long enough to accomplish their goals. That is why I am a firm believer in consistently feeding yourself for personal growth.

Many people have said to me, "Chris, you are going to teach another motivational topic.... Don't you know that, after a while, the people will go back to normal?"

My response to that is, "Of course! I know that people will eventually go back to the way they were, but that is why they need constant motivation. You don't take a shower once and say, 'That's it.' You make the same effort to stay physically clean as you do to stay highly motivated."

Here's a list of things I recommend to you to stay on a path of personal growth:

» **READ BOOKS**—Find books that motivate you and keep you growing, and read them.

- » **LISTEN TO PODCASTS**—Find your favorite speakers and listen to them over and over until their message gets down into your spirit.
- » **ATTEND SEMINARS**—Make it a habit to attend at least three to four seminars per year. These events will help charge you up and keep you going.
- » **ASSOCIATE WITH MOTIVATED PEOPLE**—I've mentioned this before, but it bears repeating. You become like those you associate with. If you want to stay motivated, associate with motivated people.
- » **SPIRITUAL RENEWAL**—For me, one of the greatest forms of motivation comes from my deep faith in God, who is my #1 source of motivation. If God isn't part of your life, you should deeply consider it. He can do far more in your life than you ever imagined.

Make personal growth a lifetime journey. Never stop learning and growing. It will keep you motivated as you conquer each step toward Higher Ground.

Stay Motivated by Motivating Others

Jaime Escalante was a teacher at Garfield High School in East Los Angeles and is the man behind the movie *Stand and Deliver*.[30] His story is one of inspiration and hope. Garfield High had been known for its violence, graffiti, and gang members filled with underachievers and led by a principal who didn't understand what it took to bring out the best in his students. In the fall of 1978, Escalante searched throughout the 3,500 students of Garfield High to establish the first calculus class. He was able to round up fourteen students to take the class and prepare for the Advanced

Placement (AP) exam. After much work, only five students took the AP exam, and only two passed.

> # YOUR LIFE HAS PURPOSE, AND THERE ARE DREAMS THAT ONLY YOU CAN LIVE OUT.

In 1980, he did it again and managed to get fifteen students for his calculus class, and this time, fourteen passed. He worked before and after school with these students year after year, believing the best in them and in their ability to succeed. In 1983, he helped thirty-one students pass the AP exam, and in 1987, 129 students took the exam with eighty-five receiving college credit. This former school of Mexican-American underachievers had now produced 27 percent of all passing AP exams in the entire United States.

Jaime Escalante is the perfect example of someone climbing for Higher Ground even in the face of difficulty. He had every right to lose his motivation and give up. . . . many of us would have. But he stayed motivated because he realized the power of motivating others. You see, you achieve your own goals when you bring out the best in them and help them achieve theirs. You've heard it said, "You get out of life what you put into it." Sink great motivation into the lives of others, and you will get great motivation out of life. You want to stay motivated? Commit to motivating others.

STAY MOTIVATED BY HOW YOU FEEL

There is something to be said for the statement "dress for success," but success isn't only about how you dress; it's about how you feel. When in peak shape, your physical body and appearance make you feel good. When someone comes up to you and says, "Have you been losing weight?" how does that make you feel? It makes you feel great. When someone comes up to you and says, "Is that a new shirt? I really like those shoes you're wearing," your spirits are lifted.

The exact opposite is also true: if you're unhappy with your appearance, it can negatively impact your emotions and serve as a de-motivator. It robs you of staying motivated and on top of your game. One of the things I like to do when I have an extra special speaking engagement is buy something new—maybe a tie, a new pair of socks, or a shirt. I buy something that makes me feel good when I put it on. If you want to stay motivated, choose to feel good. Exercise, dress nice, and display success in your appearance, and you will find it easier to stay motivated on your journey to the top.

Whatever you have to do to stay motivated, do it. Read books, listen to podcasts, attend seminars, associate with motivated people, think motivating thoughts, speak motivationally, or place motivational statements around your home, office, or in your car. However you do it is up to you, but choose to stay motivated. Your life has purpose, and there are dreams that only you can live out. They have been placed in your heart, and you are the one that destiny has called to fulfill this purpose. Don't be a quitter; stay focused and motivated on the task at hand. Here's the encouragement: motivation is a teachable quality. You can develop it if it isn't innate for you. But, to do its work, you have to be coachable and willing.

I came across this poem called "Don't Quit." I challenge you to rewrite it and place it where you can see it every day. Let it be the anthem to never ever stop.

DON'T QUIT

When things go wrong, as they sometimes will,
When the road you're trudging seems all uphill.
When the funds are low and the debts are high,
And you want to smile but you have to sigh.
When care is pressing you down a bit—
Rest if you must, but don't you quit.
Life is [strange] with its twists and turns.
As everyone of us sometimes learns.
And many a fellow turns about
When he might have won had he stuck it out.
Don't give up though the pace seems slow—
You may succeed with another blow. . . .
Success is failure turned inside out—
The silver tint of the clouds of doubt,
And when you never can tell how close you are,
It may be near when it seems afar;
So stick to the fight when you're hardest hit—
It's when things seem worse that you must not quit.[31]

CHAPTER 6

DEVELOPING THE HABITS THAT WILL TAKE YOU TO THE TOP

In February of 1998, in Nagano, Japan, the most highly trained athletes arrived for the biggest sporting event in the world...the Olympics. The Olympics is the only time when the whole world unites under the spirit of competition. Athletes, who have trained all their lives in hopes of winning the gold, come to compete with people from foreign countries—not speaking the same dialect—but speaking the same language of excellence in their sport.

America was hopeful to win several medals in various events throughout the Winter Olympics. Of all the sporting events and athletes, America's eyes seemed to turn toward two very young and competitive individuals in ladies' figure skating. Tara Lipinski, age fifteen, and Michelle Kwan, age seventeen, were highly favored to medal in their event, but the question came down to who would win the gold.

As they often do in the Olympics, brief biographies of Tara Lipinski and Michelle Kwan were given throughout the competition. These biographies would tell of the rigorous schedules that these young ladies had to keep—waking up at 4:00 a.m. and training for two to three hours before school, then training for another three to four hours after school, completing their homework before bed, only to wake up in the morning and do it again.

Their training included running, skating, eating right, and working out—a regimen they repeated day in and day out, week after week, month after month, and year after year. Their training never stopped. They realized that in order to win the gold, there was a price to be paid. If you wanted to stand on the platform and hear your country's anthem ring with the gold around your neck, you would have to keep a schedule and routine that others were unwilling to do.

In their biographies, the schedules and routines seemed similar—both worked very hard and sacrificed greatly—but I noticed something in the personal interviews. Tara Lipinski said that she had dreamed of standing on the platform with the gold. She had thought about it every day for the past several years. It was a passion inside of her that she could not escape. I noticed something different in the interview with Michelle Kwan. When asked about her expectations regarding a gold medal, she said that she was just happy to be at the Olympics, and she would see what would happen from there—a vastly different response from Tara Lipinski's, who literally dreamed of winning the gold for years. They both had outstanding work habits, but the habit of dreaming, believing, and expecting seemed to be the distinguishing factor between the two. The result was that Tara Lipinski walked away with the gold, and Michelle Kwan received the silver.

Habits are a big part of the level of success an Olympian will experience, and they will play a major role in your success as you journey to Higher Ground. The ability to create the right working habits may be the single most important tool you will need. As I have discovered for myself in my journey, the right working habits will eventually produce the results I seek. In his book *Know Your Limits—Then Ignore Them*, John Mason writes, "People spend half their time telling you what they are going to do and the other half making excuses why they didn't do it."[32] I couldn't agree with that more! But if I may be so bold, I'd like to add this: one of the reasons people don't complete what they say they will complete is that they have not developed the necessary habits to get it done. They set out with good intentions to accomplish a certain task or obtain a heartfelt dream, but they don't develop the habits necessary to see those dreams become reality.

Failing to develop the right habits is as foolish as a fitness expert failing to eat right or a boxer setting out to win the championship without having cultivated the work habits to get him there. Maybe your Higher Ground includes buying a house, early retirement, changing careers, starting a business, learning a second language or a new instrument, becoming a leader, or founding an organization. Whatever worthwhile dream you possess will only be achieved when you develop the right habits. Ignoring this principle will set you up for failure every time.

> **PEOPLE SPEND HALF THEIR TIME TELLING YOU WHAT THEY ARE GOING TO DO AND THE OTHER HALF MAKING EXCUSES WHY THEY DIDN'T DO IT.**

FACTS ABOUT HABITS

Truth 1: Good Habits Are Hard to Make

Have you ever made a New Year's resolution to begin eating right or exercising daily, only to find yourself right back where you started in less than a month? I was speaking to a friend of mine who oversees several fitness centers, and I could not believe how many people he told me were members at each fitness center.

I asked him, "Why do you sign up so many people? There is no way they could fit in here if they all came at the same time."

He said, "We count on the majority of them to not follow through with their commitment to working out."

I thought to myself, *Isn't that amazing?* The success of this fitness center is dependent on the average American's inability to follow through.

Good habits are a lot like a stamp—they are only good when they stick to something. Good habits are good, but their value and worth come from the ability to stick with them. That is why so many people start with the right idea but can't finish the job because good habits are hard to make. If they were easy, everyone would be doing them. Dream builders—people like you—must be willing to take the time and effort to instill good habits into their lives.

Take a moment to complete the exercise below. Write down one thing you would like to accomplish on the "goal" side (purchase a home, start a business, get in shape, etc.). On the "habits" side, write down the habits necessary to see this task completed.

For instance, if you want to purchase a home, you may need to create the good habit of budgeting, saving, and cutting back.

Or, if you want to get in shape, you may need to write down good eating habits and daily exercise. Complete this exercise before going any further in this chapter.

GOAL:	NECESSARY HABITS TO ACCOMPLISH THE GOAL:
1.	1.
2.	2.
3.	3.

Truth 2: Bad Habits Are Hard to Break

Not only are bad habits hard to break, but they are also a lot easier to make than good habits. Simple things, like biting your nails, become a habit that is difficult to break. But other habits become part of our lives that cost us a lot more than biting our nails. These bad habits steal from our dreams, time, and finances. Horace Mann once said, "Habit is a cable. We weave a thread of it every day, and at last we cannot break it."[33] These bad habits include:

- » Overspending
- » Overeating
- » Watching too much TV
- » Spending too much time online
- » Procrastinating
- » Smoking
- » Drinking

... and the list goes on.

The price to break these habits is high but not nearly as high as the price we pay to keep them. You always pay a price for staying the same!

I once read about the settlers who came to live in the Western US. In those days, roads were often just wagon trails. The heavy use of wagons made these trails grow very deep, so they posed serious problems for those who attempted to journey on them. A sign posted on one of the windy paths read: "Avoid this rut, or you'll be in it for the next twenty-five miles!" Isn't that a lot like a bad habit? We practice them without realizing the serious problem they will impose. Just like the wagon, we can't go down another path until we get out of the one we are in. Bad habits are hard to break, but they must be broken for anyone who wants to climb the path to Higher Ground.

SUCCESSFUL PEOPLE ARE SIMPLY WILLING TO DEVELOP THE HABITS THAT UNSUCCESSFUL PEOPLE ARE UNWILLING TO DEVELOP.

Truth 3: The Right Habits Separate

There is nothing that separates successful people from unsuccessful people more than habits. I have found that successful people are simply willing to develop the habits that unsuccessful people are unwilling to develop. One of the greatest, if not the greatest basketball legend of all time, is Michael Jordan. He is an incredible athlete, an outstanding competitor, a leader, and a team player. It has been said that Michael Jordan made it a "habit" to spend an hour or more practicing free throws after everyone else had already left practice. It was this habit that assisted him in becoming a legend. That's what the right habits do—they separate the good from the great, the ordinary from the extraordinary.

The slogan for PaineWebber & Co., an 1881 investment bank and stock brokerage firm, was "invest with discipline." Their idea is that if you make it a habit to invest with discipline regularly, over time you will become financially secure. The right habits make a difference. If you can create the habit of reading fifteen minutes per day on a self-improvement book or a book on the area you want to grow in, imagine how much you would learn after only one year. The right habits make a difference. What if you decided to make exercise a habit but only did it for twenty minutes per day. Would it make a difference? Of course, it would! The right habits always make a difference!

What if you developed the habit of showing up to work thirty minutes early every day? You would get more done and make a tremendous impression on your supervisor. What if you developed the habit of writing two encouraging notes per day to people who you work with, like colleagues, friends, future clients, mentors, or anyone else in your life? Would it make a difference? Absolutely! What if you got in the habit of making a to-do list at the end of each day and actually completed the items on the list the following day? Would it make a difference? Of course, it would!

The right habits, when regularly practiced, will eventually become second nature. Repetition has a way of creating a lifestyle out of incremental, consistent daily changes. They will set you apart from the pack; they will cause you to excel. The right habits will lift you slowly and surely to a new level in your life. Like a flower in the garden, you plant a seed and water it daily. Your habit of nurturing is necessary for the life of that potential flower. After much consistent and daily care, you will eventually reap the rewards of your work and a flower will blossom. The same is true with your dreams. Plant them in your heart, water them with the right habits, and eventually they will produce something beautiful in your life. That's the power of habits.

You now understand how the right habits can connect you to your dreams and how bad habits can keep you from your dreams. Now it's time to look at some practical suggestions that can help you rid yourself of bad habits and develop the life-changing practice of good habits.

SEEK AN ACCOUNTABILITY PARTNER

What is accountability? Accountability is being responsible for finishing what you said you would. If you open up a charge account or take out a loan, you are "accountable" for that loan or that charge account. You are responsible for whatever payment is due. Your accountability partner is, in this case, the bank. They will hold you accountable to finish what you said you would. That's accountability, and that's what an accountability partner does—they hold you to your word.

SOMETIMES YOU HAVE TO CHOOSE BETWEEN WHAT IS GOOD AND WHAT IS BEST!

If you are going to commit to creating the right habits in your life that will lead you to Higher Ground, you will need to find yourself an accountability partner, someone you trust who wants the best for you and will take the time and effort to keep you accountable. Accountability partners don't just happen. They don't knock on your door one day and say, "Hey, I would like to hold you accountable." You must seek them out and approach them, or you will never have an accountability partner.

A few years ago, I did this exact thing; I found someone whom I trust and who I know wants what's best for my life, and I asked him if he would hold me accountable. I am the one responsible for setting the meetings and being willing to speak truthfully and listen to the sometimes hard truths about areas of my life that need improvement. This person has become a close friend and mentor, and I am farther along in life because I continuously seek him out for accountability.

Begin thinking about someone who could become your accountability partner. Make sure it is someone you know will be truthful with you. Share your dreams, goals, and aspirations with this individual. Show them your plan and the habits necessary to obtain your goals, and have them keep you accountable to these new habits. Similar to a nutrition consultant who keeps you accountable and on track with your fitness goal, that's what your accountability partner will do for you.

TODAY IS THE TOMORROW THAT YOU SAID YESTERDAY YOU WOULD GET IT DONE.

ELIMINATE TIME WASTERS

According to research, the smallest change in your dietary habits can make a big difference in overall health. In one study, the authors found that small changes in diet and exercise led to significantly improved weight management outcomes,[34] presumably because weight gain has been found to occur gradually over time.[35] Another study found that BMI significantly lowered over fourteen weeks in children who replaced sugar with artificial sweeteners.[36] A separate study yielded similar outcomes in a separate study—children who increased their steps to 2,000 each day compared to children in the control group either maintained or decreased BMI over a six-month period.[37]

What's the point? Small changes—schedule adjustments, calorie dosing changes, you name it—are not a waste of time. Not even close! It's true with food, and it's true with your daily life. The key is to narrow down the list of what I call "time wasters." Take a moment to figure out what wastes your time and keeps you from developing habits necessary for success. Keep in mind that time wasters are not always bad—sometimes, they are *good* activities, like volunteering or participating in community events. They may help you recharge, reset, and even serve others. But, if they suck your energy or distract you from those things that are most important to you, then they aren't serving you well. Sometimes, you have to choose between what is good and what is best!

Take some time to think this through. What are the time wasters in your life? They could be as simple as binging on TV or habitually scrolling on your phone. Whatever they may be, they will keep you from spending time developing the habits necessary for your growth.

When I started South Hills Community Church in Corona, California, I was heavily involved with another organization that my good friend, Donny Burleson, led. This organization is called On Fire, and its purpose is to speak into the lives of teenagers across America through our public school system. On Fire speaks about topics such as peer pressure, making the right choices, and living drug and alcohol-free. This is a great organization, and I was honored to be a part of it; however, when my wife and I began the process of planting a brand new church, this endeavor took much of our time, so much so that I was forced to pull back from On Fire. Is speaking in schools a bad thing? Of course not. It just wasn't the best thing for my life at that time.

That's what you have to do. You have to decide what habits are necessary for you to achieve your dreams. Then you have to make a list of what activities, good or bad, need to be cut back or removed altogether to have more time for the habits that are right for you.

DO AT LEAST ONE THING A DAY YOU DON'T WANT TO DO

There are so many things in our daily routines that we know we need to do but continually put off. We may need to call someone we don't want to, finish a project that we don't fully enjoy, or face an inevitable confrontation, but we continue to wait just one more day. Phone calls don't get made, meetings go unscheduled, paperwork piles up, and to-do items always make the list the next day. Some things help us succeed, allow us to be more effective at our jobs, and even create growth in our personal lives, but we say, "I'll take care of that 'one of these days.'" As you well know, "one of these days" really means "none of these days." I read once, "Today is the tomorrow that you said yesterday you would get done."

I am not someone who likes to waste time. I enjoy productivity. But just like you, I am committed to doing certain things every day of my life. Each morning, I shave, shower, iron my clothes, brush my teeth, comb my hair, and get ready for the day. As silly as this may sound to you, all of that bores me. I think about the thirty to forty-five minutes per day it takes to accomplish these tasks—the 5.25 hours per week totaling 273 hours per year that I could be doing something else. Some things just aren't our favorite things to do, but we have to do them. I encourage you to develop the "right habit" of doing at least one thing per day that you know you need to do but keep putting off. Do this, and it will help you become the person you dream of being.

MAKE SUCCESS A HABIT

My final challenge to you to develop the right habits is to make "success" a regular habit in your life. Something extraordinary happens with each win you put underneath your belt. The wins create momentum, and that momentum becomes the fuel that propels you up the mountain toward Higher Ground. In the 2001 NBA playoffs, the Los Angeles Lakers had won fifteen straight games and seemed unstoppable. In the championship series, they lost the first game to the Philadelphia 76ers. This was a huge upset for the Lakers and their fans. No one expected them to lose. Everyone had anticipated the Lakers to sweep the game. People had gained such confidence in the Lakers because "success" had become a habit for them. They were used to winning, and the fans were used to seeing them win.

That's what the habit of success does. It gives you confidence and momentum that makes you unstoppable. If you want to be successful, discover the power of making success a habit. For you, it may be completing certain projects by the end of the month or reaching a financial goal by the end of the year. It may mean starting something you've said you would start but still haven't. If you can do these things and do them with excellence, you will begin to gain the confidence that comes from making success a habit.

As I said at the beginning of this chapter, habits may possibly be the most important tool for your success. You may not notice the difference right away, but eventually you will. Developing the right habits will ultimately lead you to achieve all your dreams and goals. The right habits are the difference between first and second, gold and silver, success and failure. Change your habits from what is good to what is best and from what hinders you to what helps you, and ultimately, you will find yourself at a level you once thought impossible!

CHAPTER 7

HIGHER GROUND BECOMES SHAKY GROUND WITHOUT THE BALANCE OF SOLID GROUND

PART 1

I hope this book has inspired and challenged you to continually reach for Higher Ground. I believe in the human spirit and that everyone is loaded with potential and ability to accomplish great things. I believe in people's abilities so much that I have dedicated my life to helping them discover the possibilities that lie within them. However, I must admit that over the years, I have met many people who have pursued Higher Ground and reached a level of success that many others desire, but they are unhappy. They have a business that's thriving, financial security, and many personal achievements, but it still seems their life is lacking. Why is that? Why is it that some people seem to have it all, but still seem to have nothing?

Probably because most people connect the word "success" with the word "money." When we see someone who is financially independent, we automatically judge that person as "successful." Money can buy a lot of enjoyable things, but success cannot be limited to those things. Success must include the things money cannot buy. It has been said that money can:

1) Buy a bed, but not sleep,
2) Buy affection, but not love,
3) Buy company, but not friends,
4) Buy a wedding, but not a marriage, and
5) Buy a house, but not a home.

I was recently having lunch with a friend who shared some sad news regarding a mutual friend whom I'll call "Mike." Mike has had a great level of success in many areas of his life. He was not born into a wealthy family but decided at a young age that he was going to make something of himself. In his early twenties, he began working for someone else on the weekends while running a small retail business. Over a few years, this business began to grow so much that he was able to quit his weekend job and devote himself entirely to his business. He worked hard and dedicated all his time and efforts, and year after year, it continued to pay off in great dividends.

He expanded his small shop and began to build his own place. Soon he was operating his business from a 33,000-square-foot shop as he began to see his business hit a new level of success. Over time, he diversified his work across multiple projects including real estate, and each project brought him success. Everything he touched turned to gold. Mike was an entrepreneur and an icon in the city where he lived. The sad news was that Mike had been diagnosed with a disease, and his chance of survival was slim. After hearing this news, I drove back to my office and began to think about his life. Death always causes you to think about life.

I asked myself, *Was Mike a success?* Then I realized you can't answer that question until you define success. So, I first thought about his finances. Undoubtedly, he is a success when it comes to money. He is a multimillionaire and has enjoyed all the things that life has to offer—vacations, houses, big cars, country clubs—anything he wants, he can have. I thought about his career. Was he a success? There was no doubt about this either. Mike has lived out the American dream. He did not come from a wealthy or affluent family, but he worked hard and remained dedicated, and as a result, his business was a thriving success. Then I began to think about his personal life. He had one failed marriage, and his marriage at the time was on the rocks. Mike seemed to have worked so hard to make a living that he had forgotten to make a life.

I also thought about his children. Each of them has had their fair share of personal struggles. Drug abuse, illegitimate children, and a low standard of values and morals are all part of their stories. I am not saying that Mike was a bad parent or that his children didn't love him. What I am saying is that, to a certain degree, Mike did not fulfill his biggest parenting obligation—raising his children with a deep level of character. There was no spiritual awareness in his life and nothing of true value passed on to his children.

ALWAYS MAKE SURE YOU HAVE SOMETHING TO GO HOME TO.

Then I thought about the disease that was taking over his body, and I couldn't help but wonder what words would be said at his funeral should he die. I wondered about the legacy and heritage he would leave. Had he done anything in his life that would outlast him? I thought about the words of Ralph Waldo Emerson when he spoke of the true picture of success.

> To laugh often and much; to win the respect of intelligent people and the affection of children; to earn the

appreciation of honest critics and endure the betrayal of false friends; to appreciate the beauty; to find the best in others; to leave the world a bit better, whether by a healthy child, a garden patch or a redeemed social condition; to know even one life has breathed easier because you have lived. This is to have succeeded![38]

Now that you have a clearer picture of Mike, what do you think? Does money make him successful?

Don't get me wrong; money is a great thing and can be used for great purposes, but you cannot classify money as the means for success. You see, Mike had a dream. He wanted to create a successful business and make lots of money, and he did. However, one thing Mike forgot to do was to keep his feet on "solid ground" while reaching for Higher Ground. Mike had forgotten the golden rule behind the principle of Higher Ground: "Higher Ground becomes Shaky Ground without the balance of Solid Ground."

REPUTATION IS WHAT OTHERS THINK YOU ARE, AND CHARACTER IS WHAT YOU REALLY ARE.

Consider the courageous people called tightrope walkers. They stand on a thin rope suspended high in the air, and they walk across from one side to the other. The key to the entire success of that tightrope walker is one word—"balance." His entire life is dependent on his ability to keep things in balance. The same is true for anyone seeking Higher Ground. Their entire success depends on balance.

Whatever Higher Ground you reach will always be incomplete without balance. Success cannot be limited to financial security, writing a book, starting a business, or even fulfilling a dream. Success is always more than this. I have had the honor to sit and chat with the Chief of Police for the city of Corona. His name is Richard Gonzales, and he does an outstanding job with our police force. He tells his staff and police officers, "Always make sure you have something to go home to." In other words, it does not matter how successful we are in one area of our lives; success has to contain more than just our careers.

Imagine a large wagon wheel that has various spokes extending out from the center. The ability to make a wheel roll properly lies in the balance. The strength and success of that wheel rely on the balance of the spokes. Let's pretend that your life is that wheel, and the spokes in the wheel represent various areas in your life, including personal, financial, relational, physical, emotional, professional, mental, and spiritual. The success of your life depends on your success in each of these areas. In this chapter, I want to break down the first four elements for you and provide some practical ideas that will help you raise the bar of excellence in each category. (I will discuss the last four elements in the following chapter.) Remember, the goal is not to say, "Well, four out of eight ain't bad." The goal is to find yourself pursuing each of these areas and arrive at a new level of success.

PERSONAL

The first spoke in your wheel is the "person" spoke. This is your character—who you are when no one is looking. It is the premise of your true success as a person, leader, worker, spouse, parent, or friend. Have you ever heard someone say, "That person is a real character," about someone else? People often say this in reference to various aspects of a person's character—humorous, fun to be around, or maybe just unique. But, in truth, "that person is a real character" usually describes that person's reputation, not their character. Reputation is what others think you are, and character is what you really are. Character is what really matters.

Some people may think character doesn't matter. If it's only what you are when no one is looking, then who cares? It won't affect my business, my family, or my finances if no one knows. Nothing could be further from the truth! If character doesn't matter, tell that to the person who just found out their spouse is having a secret affair, to the person who just discovered their accountant has been skimming from the top, or to the person whose business partner has left the country with all their money. I promise you this—character matters to those people.

Have you ever heard of the Boy Scouts oath? It reads, "On my honor, I will do my best to do my duty to God and my country and obey the Scout Law; to help other people at all times; to keep myself physically strong, mentally awake, and morally straight." Following the oath, the Boy Scouts repeat the Scout's motto, which is, "Be prepared," and the Scout's law, which is, "A Scout is trustworthy, loyal, helpful, friendly, courteous, kind, obedient, cheerful, thrifty, brave, clean, and reverent."[39] These sound like wonderful things. Unfortunately, I never belonged to the Boy

Scouts. It was something, quite frankly, that I thought was for sissies. I realized how wrong I was later in life, especially when I came across this recent statistic.

In 2005, Harris Interactive studied adult males who had spent a minimum of five years in Boy Scouts. Their findings showed that Scouts scored higher on a range of traits and values that reflect integrity and honesty (e.g., trustworthiness, loyalty, helpfulness). Compared to 87 percent of non-Scouts, 91 percent of Scouts completed high school, and 35 percent finished college (compared to 19 percent of those who were not Scouts). Scouts were also found to earn an average of $80,000 dollars annually compared to $61,000 for men who were not Scouts.[40]

As of 2023, 85 percent of student council presidents, 64 percent of Air Force Academy graduates, 58 percent of West Point graduates, 85 percent of FBI agents, and 57.4 percent of astronauts were former Boy Scouts.[41]

I'D RATHER HAVE ROSES ON MY TABLE THAN DIAMONDS AROUND MY NECK.

Living the life of a Boy Scout pays off! Honesty, courtesy, kindness, integrity, loyalty, friendliness, and genuine, true character are the premise behind the Boy Scouts and ultimately the means for their personal success. Thomas Jefferson once said, "Whenever you are to do a thing, though it can never be known but to yourself, ask yourself how you would act were all the world looking at you, and act accordingly."[42] Remember, there are many things in life that others can take from you—a family, a fortune or even health. Character, however, is the one thing that cannot be taken from you . . . but you can give it away.

FINANCIAL

The next spoke on your wagon wheel is "financial." Finances are a big part of our society and often used as a measuring stick for where you're at in life. Finances are not everything. . .but they are something. If you want a home, a car, or to take a nice vacation, you'll need finances. If you want to send your children to college or help them get into their first house, you'll need finances. Finances are great as an assistance to you and your family. I'm not talking about becoming a millionaire—though I'm sure most of us wouldn't mind that—but we already know that finances cannot be the source of true happiness. I'm talking about the one word this entire chapter is centered around . . . balance. We must bring balance to our finances.

THE AVERAGE SENIOR CITIZEN RETIRED WITH LESS THAN EIGHTY-SEVEN DOLLARS IN THEIR PERSONAL SAVINGS.

If you live in America, you live in a country that is full of opportunity. No other place in the world is like America. A nice home, car, job, college education, or relatively decent level of financial security is available to anyone who wants it. The problem lies not in opportunity or availability but in our failure to properly manage the finances we are given.

In her book *Work, Retire, Repeat,* Teresa Ghilarducci found that "only 10 percent of Americans between the ages of 62 and 70 are both retired and financially stable."[43] Bankrate's 2025 Annual Emergency Savings Report found that in 2024, over a quarter (27 percent) of US adults had no emergency savings, while just 16 percent could cover three to five months of living expenses.[44] As of 2023, the average person had five credit card accounts, paying $473.85 in interest and fees on average,[45] and the 2025 credit card debt in America is outrageously high—$1.166 trillion dollars![46] None of these facts have anything to do with the economy in America but everything to do with people improperly managing the finances they do have.

Your Higher Ground may not include finances. It may be to raise wonderful children, to learn a second language, to develop as a leader, or to be the founder of a non-profit organization. Whatever your personal Higher Ground is, you must include the powerful benefit of properly managing your finances. I strongly encourage you to discuss your financial future with an expert. Develop a plan to pay off your home or fund your future, your retirement, your college education, or any other dream. You might be saying, "But I don't make a lot of money." It doesn't take as much as you think. Sit down with a financial planner, and you will discover the power of budgeting your finances and consistently investing in your future.

RELATIONAL

We now arrive at the third spoke in the wheel that will help keep your life in balance—your relationships. All the personal success in the world won't mean anything if you don't have someone to share it with. Unfortunately, people pursue their personal Higher Ground at the cost of their relationships. Marriages lose their romance, children lose touch with their parents, and families become fragmented under the guidelines of success at any cost. We are a society in desperate need of turning our attention to the family. What good does it do to have all the money in the world if your marriage is failing or to have a thriving business at the price of becoming more of a guardian than a parent?

I find great truth in what Yvonne de Gaulle, wife of the French President, once said, "The presidency is temporary—but the family is permanent."[47] Or what Emma Goldman stated regarding the family, "I'd rather have roses on my table, than diamonds around my neck."[48] These great women, with all their accomplishments and financial security, have realized something that takes others a lifetime to realize: true success is impossible without successful relationships. A spouse that you love more each day, children to laugh and play with, and genuine friends with whom you can share your life are commodities that success cannot live without.

I live in Southern California and life is always moving quickly. I have a business to run, a church to pastor, grandchildren to love, and people who want "a moment" of my time. Just like you,

I am extremely busy. Although we never intend it to, this word called "busyness" robs us of our relationships. It's quite easy to let it happen in life, primarily because the things we are busy with are often good things and noble activities. However, these events that fill our calendars, regardless of how wonderful they may be, slowly deteriorate our relationships with others. Those closest to us are left feeling like the "runner up" in a race they never wanted to compete in.

Author Max Lucado wrote some wonderful thoughts on how busyness affects our relationships. Here's a paraphrased version of what he wrote:

> *Busyness is an expert in robbing the sparkle and replacing it with the drab. Busyness invented the yawn and put the hum in humdrum. The strategy of busyness is deceptive! With the passing of time, he'll infiltrate your heart with fatigue and cover the cross with dust so you will be safely out of the reach of change.*
>
> *Busyness won't steal your marriage from you. He'll do something far worse; he'll paint it with a familiar coat of drabness. He'll replace evening gowns with bathrobes, nights on the town with evenings in the recliner and romance with routine. He'll scatter the dust of yesterday over the wedding pictures in the hallway until they become a memory of another couple, in another time. Hence, walks won't be taken, games will go unplayed, hearts will go unnurtured, opportunities for intimacy will go ignored. All because the poison of busyness has blinded your eyes to the wonder of your spouse.*[49]

Throughout the course of my life, I have heard people speak with deep regret. Regret for not nurturing their marriage, regret for not spending enough time with their children, and regret for not having enough people in their lives they call "friends." Although relationships are only one spoke in your wheel of life, that spoke is an important one. Keep your life in balance by keeping in mind what really matters!

PHYSICAL

I have already spent some time discussing the importance of physical health, so I will not spend too much time here again. Let me just say that I am by no means the expert on physical health, but I do try my best to stay in shape and eat right. I have got a long way to go, but I am working on it. One thing I do know is that exercising and eating right positively affects your approach and perspective on life. It gives you more energy, boosts your self-confidence, and causes you to embrace and enjoy life at a higher level. Oddly enough, I seem to get more done with less hours on the days I work out.

A lack of physical activity will limit the height of your Higher Ground. Get active, feel better about yourself, and set a plan of action now! Make it a priority to stay in shape, and your overall success will reach new heights. Nothing compares to the confidence you feel when you look in the mirror and are proud of what you see.

CHAPTER 8

HIGHER GROUND BECOMES SHAKY GROUND WITHOUT THE BALANCE OF SOLID GROUND

PART 2

In the previous chapter, we explored the first four of eight elements, or spokes on our wheel, that must move quickly and freely in order to keep our life in balance:

» Personal
» Financial
» Relational
» Physical

Your personal Higher Ground is dependent upon your ability to keep these items balanced in your life, but there are more!

Some would argue that the eight elements are an either/or choice. In other words, if you are completely committed to your family life, then you will not have financial success. Or if you are committed to your career, your family will suffer. I couldn't disagree more! I do not believe that the eight spokes of life are an either/or choice. I am convicted to believe that all of them are possible given hard work and balance. I believe with all my heart that each person can live with a high level of character, that their relationships can be rewarding and fulfilling, that they can obtain a comfortable level of financial independence, and that they can be emotionally, mentally, and physically healthy while maintaining a constant and growing faith in God. Life is not an either/or because Higher Ground does not have to exist in only one area of your life. If you are at least willing to be all that your Creator wants you to be, more and better is always possible.

We have discovered the first four elements or spokes in our lives. Now, let's take a look at the final four elements that are necessary to keep our wheels rolling.

EMOTIONAL

We are speaking here primarily of freedom from emotional baggage. We live in a society where emotional baggage is easy to pick up. There are millions of people who are bitter toward a former spouse, angry at a parent who neglected them, have memories of a tragedy that took place in their life, have a friend who hurt or betrayed them, or have had a certain event that has caused them to live with constant resentment. This type of baggage is like a giant weight attached to your heart, and it keeps you from climbing to Higher Ground.

Anybody who knows me knows that I always say, "The events in your life can make you 'bitter' or 'better.'" The choice is up to you. Unfortunately, many people choose to walk around with a chip on their shoulder. Something or someone has hurt them, and they just can't let it go. They hold on to this bitterness or resentment as if holding will somehow change the outcome. I have learned that resentment is like a boomerang. It keeps coming back and hitting you upside the head. I also have learned that most of the time, those whom we are resentful toward don't know it and quite often don't care.

As I continue to climb up my own Higher Ground, I have had my share of darts thrown at me. People have hurt me in ways I would have never expected. Sometimes, the people in whom I had personally invested my life have said the most hurtful things of all. I can choose to let it make me bitter, or I can choose to let it make me better. I choose the latter! I don't want to live with resentment. I realize that my Higher Ground will be extremely limited if I cannot learn to let it go. I agree with Lady Margaret Thatcher, who is widely credited with saying, "The secret of my success has been in my ability to not waste time with regrets." In the same way the former Prime Minister of Britain does not waste time on regrets, I do not want to waste time with resentment. J.P. Vaswani once said, "It's wise to remember that anger is just one letter short of danger."[50]

> **RESENTMENT IS LIKE A BOOMERANG. IT KEEPS COMING BACK AND HITTING YOU UPSIDE THE HEAD.**

Please note that I do not want to minimize events that have hurt you. In my line of work, I meet hundreds of people with real pain from real situations. I feel for them, and I do my best to help them overcome it. I want to do the same for you. If there is resentment, anger, or bitterness in your life, you have to deal with it. See a counselor or pastor, but begin to remove that thing that is wrapped around your heart and won't let you go. If you don't, you are destined to live a life short of your capabilities. You will never reach your Highest Ground because you will be anchored by a weight called resentment, and it will inhibit you from climbing to the top. Be determined to conquer your emotional baggage, or in the end, it will conquer you!

PROFESSIONAL

Years ago, a movie premiered starring Billy Crystal called *City Slickers*. The main character was your typical middle-aged man. He had a good job, a wife, two children, and was making decent money. However, he had become bored with his life and bored with his work. His job performance was so poor that his boss demanded to approve any decision he would make. Then, his two buddies gave him a gift for his birthday—a two-week adventure in which they would move a herd of cows from Colorado to Texas. (I know what you are thinking: *That doesn't sound like much fun.*)

The movie is great and full of comedy, but when he sees his wife again at the end of the movie, she says to him, "I have been thinking; if you want to quit your job because you are not happy, go ahead, we'll get by."

He says to her, "No, I'm not going to quit, I'm just going to do it better."[51]

Maybe you can identify with Billy Crystal's character and the thousands of other Americans who say, "I hate my job." Maybe it's not the job you want or maybe it's a job until you finish schooling or until your business gets off the ground. Either way, it's what you do to make a living and where you probably spend about a third of your life. What you may not realize is that someone who is reaching for Higher Ground is also someone who does the best they can in any situation. Every mountain you climb has its share of obstacles. That's what makes it a mountain. It's your attitude toward the obstacles that will make all the difference in your journey to the top.

No matter where you are or what you may be doing—whether you're the CEO of a major company or a trash collector—you must set out to be the best you can be. Your occupation may not be what you want at this time, but that is not the point. Your attitude toward your current profession will be the same attitude you carry with you throughout life. If you can't strive for excellence at your current level, there's a good chance that you won't be ready for the next level.

The screen on my laptop went out during the writing of this book. After discovering the cost to repair would be the same as buying a new one, I found myself going from store to store to find the best possible deal. I went into one of the national chains that sells computer equipment. I looked at all the laptops they had on display. I found a man in the aisle behind me stacking equipment on a shelf, and I jokingly asked him, "Are you the laptop man?"

Without any expression, he said, "Yes."

I said, "I have a few questions regarding your laptops on display."

IF YOU WANT TO CLIMB TO THE TOP, MAKE A SOLID FOOTPRINT WHERE YOU CURRENTLY ARE.

Without any apology, he said to me, "I'm kind of busy right now. Why don't you find someone else."

I am usually quick with a comeback, but this threw me off. I have never had a salesperson be so blunt with me and show such a lack of consideration for me as a customer.

A few things occurred to me as I drove away from the store. First, the salesman must not like his job. He must be one of the thousands of people who would rather be doing anything than what he was currently doing. Second, I felt a little sorry for the guy. He obviously does not understand that it is probably his attitude toward his job that will keep him at the current level.

His boss is unlikely to promote him. Customers are unlikely to be impressed with his people skills or offer him a job, and, most likely, he will carry forward his attitude toward his current vocation into the rest of his life.

IF YOU WANT TO MOVE FORWARD, KEEP YOUR HEAD ON STRAIGHT.

If you want to climb to the top, make a solid footprint where you currently are. Let those around you see your great attitude. Let them see that you work hard and strive for excellence in each task. There is always room at the top for those with a great attitude, quality work ethics, and superior people skills. Your approach toward your current profession will determine the outcome of your future profession. Put your promotion in motion by living with this resolve: "Whatever I do, I do my best!"

MENTAL

The next spoke in the wheel of life is "mental." The mental condition of a person strongly determines the outcome of that person's life. You are more likely to reach your Higher Ground with a healthy mind.

Doctors, psychologists, and behavioral studies all point to the power of a healthy mental approach toward life. Even the Bible indicates that our actions follow our thoughts and that if someone truly believes, they can overcome the mountains in their lives.

Good mental health promotes high self-esteem and belief in yourself and the endless possibilities available to you. It means more optimistic thinking. It is marked by the understanding that nothing good comes out of a negative mindset because the persistently pessimistic individual is without hope. In a nutshell—discouragement and negativity will never deliver, but optimism will.

I have learned many times on my way up to Higher Ground that I have to keep my head on straight if I want to move forward. I remember when the church where I pastor was in the middle of a building program. We had only been established for three years, had purchased property, and were raising funds to build. Throughout this project, there had been many difficulties—overseeing and raising millions of dollars, interactions with the city, working side by side with a project manager, and countless other twists and turns. Even listing them now feels overwhelming! I could have slipped into negativity many times. I could have gotten discouraged and lost hope. But like my good friend Chris Turner told me, "Once you have decided to climb a mountain, never, ever look back." There is no hope, no joy, no comfort, and no strength found in a negative mentality.

Martin Seligman, a psychologist at the University of Pennsylvania, has proven that optimists are more successful than equally talented pessimists in business, education, sports, and politics. Seligman and Schulman found evidence for this theory using the "Seligman Attributional Style Questionnaire." For this study, the survey aimed to distinguish between pessimists and optimists and examine the differences in total insurance sales between the two groups. They discovered that the optimistic group outsold the pessimistic group by as much as 50 percent per year.[52] Same talent and same ability but different mental outlook.

One time, I took my wife and two children on vacation. We went to Cancun, Mexico, for seven days. We had a great time. It's a beautiful place to visit, and there is so much to see. On our third day there, we went where they offered snorkeling as one of the available activities. We had heard there were magnificent fish to see in this small lagoon area, so we just had to see it for ourselves. We rented our equipment, and we were ready to go. We marched down to the lagoon, ready to explore God's creation. When we arrived, we gave our children, who were six and seven, a lesson on how to breathe through the equipment while being underwater. After our insightful instructions, we were off. Within minutes, my six-year-old son A. J. began screaming for me. He had managed to swallow some of the saltwater that accidentally got into his snorkel. From that point on, he did not want to participate. He had determined that he could not do it. For the rest of the day he didn't snorkel. A few days later, we went to another tourist sight and found an even greater place to snorkel. We begged him to try and after much persuading, he finally gave in. He loved it! He snorkeled for hours and saw the incredible sea life of Cancun, Mexico, first-hand.

I tell you this story to point out a few observations. First of all, my son became convinced that a tragedy had taken place. He had swallowed seawater. This event shook him up so much that he refused to participate anymore. Secondly, he kept telling me over and over, "I can't do it. I don't know how." He had made up his mind that he was unable to accomplish the task. Thirdly, once he got over it in his mind, he realized that he could do it, and the result was an experience he will never forget. You see, this little illustration describes our mental approach many times in our lives. Once we get it in our head that we can't do something, it's very difficult to get past it. Our mind is a powerful thing. If we would just attempt what we think is impossible, we would realize how much we would have missed had we continued with our pessimistic approach. Focus your mind on the possibilities, and your mind will direct you to a Higher Ground.

SPIRITUAL

The final spoke in the wheel of life is spiritual. For those who have a practicing faith, this is what you may call a no-brainer. You have a faith that is lived out each day, and you have come to understand the great joy and fulfillment that comes from having God in your life. But for those who have not yet consecrated their life to God or who have put their faith into action, this act of spirituality may seem irrelevant. It may be hard for you to imagine why a spiritual pursuit would be necessary for success. How does God fit into my relationships, career, finances, or any other dream or goal I am pursuing?

A variety of studies have been done indicating that having an active faith is helpful for one's day-to-day life. For instance, Ann Wilder and colleagues studied the impact of prayer on various measures of older adults' life satisfaction and discovered as the practice of prayer increased, so did self-reported life satisfaction.[53] Another study has indicated that those who put their faith in God show significantly higher levels of forgiveness, commitment to the relationship, and marital satisfaction,[54] all of which lend themselves to marital longevity. As of 2024, the odds of divorce in America is approximately 42 percent.[55] The odds for divorce among couples who attend church together are around 26 percent, and only one in 1,500 couples who actively pray together divorce.[56] Another study indicated those who practice their faith have a lower level of stress in their lives.[57] The takeaway couldn't be clearer—a strong spiritual life can change everything.

I was once asked, "How would having God in my life make a difference?" I told them that they could have a great marriage, be relatively successful, and do well financially without God in their life, but the presence of God versus the absence of God is like watching a show on HDTV as opposed to standard definition. Both show the same picture, but one is clearer, more beautiful, more colorful, and richer. That is the difference God makes.

I would encourage you to establish a practicing faith in God for yourself if you do not currently have one. Find a local church that believes in the Lord and the Bible, and begin to seek out what it really means to have an active faith in God. You will discover what millions of businessmen, political leaders, firemen, policemen, entrepreneurs, and small and big business leaders have discovered for themselves—God makes a difference.

PUTTING IT ALL TOGETHER

Before you move any further, think back over the eight spokes in the wheel of life (personal, financial, relationships, physical, emotional, professional, mental, and spiritual), and consider the ones you need to work on the most. What needs to change in your life? What priorities are out of line? Are there character issues that need to be handled or maybe some relationships that need nurturing? Maybe you have some emotional issues that need tending, or it's possible you need a boost of self-confidence and a new positive outlook to help you reach your Higher Ground. Whichever one (or more) it is, begin working on it. Don't neglect one or the other; pursue excellence in each area. Remember, the spokes only move smoothly toward the top when they are all in balance.

I said earlier in this chapter that the eight spokes in the wheel of life are not an either/or decision. In one speech, legendary motivational speaker Zig Ziglar asked this question, "How do you get more of the things money will buy and all of the things that money won't buy?" He gets to the punchline later in his speech when he says, "The more of the things that you have that money won't buy—those are the things that will enable you to get more of the things that money will buy."[58] So, balance is key. Work hard at all eight spokes and become the person you are meant to be!

CHAPTER 9

WHEN IT'S SCARY . . . DON'T LOOK DOWN

During the writing of this book, our nation—and the world—faced a crisis that will be etched in history forever. Only five years ago, the first news of a novel coronavirus began to spread. At first, it seemed distant, an event unfolding in another part of the world. Within weeks, though, it was clear that this virus—COVID-19—and its aftermath were unlike anything we had experienced in our lifetime. Borders closed, schools shut down, businesses shuttered, and hospitals reached capacity as frontline workers battled a growing pandemic.

The virus caused a dramatic upheaval that shook the foundations of our economy, communities, and daily lives. Millions of Americans were forced to adapt overnight—working remotely, homeschooling children, or, in many cases, facing sudden unemployment. The empty streets of bustling cities like New York were a haunting reminder of the uncertainty that gripped our nation. The pain was raw, and the fear was real.

Yet, in the face of chaos, uncertainty, and grief, something else emerged: courage. While the challenges of the pandemic were unprecedented, so, too, were the displays of resilience and bravery from people across all walks of life.

Healthcare workers and first responders showed incredible fortitude, working day and night to save lives, even when protective equipment was scarce. Teachers, parents, and students adjusted to virtual classrooms, redefining education on the fly. Grocery store clerks, delivery drivers, and essential workers kept life moving forward despite the risks.

These leaders understood that courage is contagious. When leaders act with courage, they empower others to face adversity head-on. We saw this reflected in communities that rallied to support their neighbors, in small businesses that reinvented themselves to stay afloat, and in individuals who found ways to create moments of joy amidst uncertainty.

The pandemic revealed cracks in systems we thought were unshakable—economic stability, supply chains, and even our sense of normalcy. But it also revealed the strength of the human spirit. The courage displayed by leaders, frontline workers, and everyday citizens in 2020 set an example for future generations. Just as America rebounded stronger after 9/11, we will rise from this as well, thanks to the bravery of those who refuse to give up.

> **FOR ANYONE WHO HAS A PERSONAL HIGHER GROUND, COURAGE IS NOT AN OPTION; IT IS A MUST.**

Courage is a great thing! For anyone who has a personal Higher Ground, courage is not an option; it is a must. Whatever mountain you are climbing, whatever dream you are dreaming, courage must be in your backpack as you journey up to this place we have called Higher Ground. Courage enables you to blast through the obstacles and opposition you will face. Courage keeps you going when nothing else will. It is the antidote to your fear and the prescription to your insecurities. Your success in life will be marked by the amount of courage you have. Without courage, this country does not have freedom. Without courage, this nation does not have peace. Without courage, electricity would not have been discovered, cars would not be driven, and airplanes would be a foreign word to you and me. Without courage, television would have never been invented, Disneyland would have never existed, companies would have never begun, and a man would have never walked on the moon. Courage built our country, and it will build your dreams and help you reach Higher Ground.

In my own life, courage has kept me going through difficult obstacles and pressures. Many times, fear grips my heart, and uncertainty of the future causes me to doubt, but it is courage that keeps me going. Courage at the very core is always the same—it does not matter who you are or what dream you are attempting to live out; courage is necessary for everyone. I'm talking about the same kind of courage it takes to be the President of the United States in times of crisis. The same kind of courage that a company owner must have to problem-solve and forge ahead when the bottom line looks bleak. The same kind of courage necessary for you to reach your highest potential or make a dream a reality. Let me break it down for you and show you how to live your life courageously on your way up to Higher Ground.

KEEP CLIMBING—EVEN WHEN YOU CAN'T SEE THE ROAD IN FRONT OF YOU

Remember that building project I mentioned? Anyone who has been part of any building project knows that several challenges are faced each day. One of the greatest challenges is finances. A great deal of money is necessary to buy land and to build. A church is a non-profit organization, so finding lenders to raise funds can become very difficult.

> **GOOD THINGS COME TO THOSE WHO WAIT—BUT ONLY WHAT'S LEFT OVER BY THOSE WHO HUSTLE.**

So many times, we had to continue our journey even though we could not see the road in front of us, like hiring architects and engineers before we owned the land, because we knew that we needed to move quickly. We had to move forward with our permit process without having all the financing in place. The list goes on and on of all the times the road was unclear, but we needed to move forward. That's where the courage to move forward came in—even when things were a little unclear. Most people make the mistake of waiting for risk-free conditions before they proceed. They create the largest safety net possible and wait for all questions to be answered before continuing their journey up the mountain. This well-known maxim is often attributed to

President Lincoln: "Things may come to those who wait, but only the things left by those who hustle."

Nothing great has been accomplished and nothing wonderful has been invented without the courage to move forward when the road ahead was uncertain. Imagine if you were to refuse to drive home until you could see the entire road. You would never leave your home! When we drive, we can only see as far as our headlights (maybe thirty to forty feet, at best). When you drive the distance your headlights can reach, you continue because now you can see another thirty to forty feet. The same principle applies to your personal Higher Ground adventure. You will never arrive at the top if you wait until the whole path is visible! You climb as far as you can go, and when it is unclear, you keep climbing. It was Mark Twain who said, "Courage is resistance to fear, mastery of fear—not absence of fear."[59] Everyone feels fear, but few move forward in spite of it. Don't let fear own you or control your destiny. Stand with courage—even when you are afraid—and keep marching upward!

COURAGE TO MAKE TOUGH DECISIONS

Every great leader, dreamer, inventor, founder or Higher Ground seeker must have the courage to make the tough decisions. Sometimes, we are blessed with the luxury of waiting, contemplating, and seeking advice. Other times, the decision must be made immediately, and we have to have the courage to make it. That is not an easy thing to do because no one wants to be wrong. However, the reality is that decision-making is part of the process for anyone on the road to Higher Ground. Former President Eisenhower nearly blew it on D-Day because of his fear of making a tough decision immediately. Before he reacted, he was quoted as saying, "No matter what the weather looks like, we have to go ahead now. Waiting any longer could be even more dangerous. So let's move it!"[60] He proved himself a great leader when he made the toughest decision in his military career—and quickly.

I've had to make countless difficult decisions throughout my life. Sometimes, I was right, but often, I have been wrong. That's just a part of decision-making—you gather the information you can, seek the available advice, and sometimes make the wrong decision—but with courage. I have found that the right decision can become wrong when it is made too late. You are not always going to be right. When you are wrong, admit it.

VALUES MUST BE STATED AND PLACED FIRMLY INTO THE FIBER OF YOUR PERSONAL AND BUSINESS LIFE.

Make corrections if possible and move forward, but do not be afraid to make the next tough decision that comes your way. T. Boone Pickens once said, "Be willing to make decisions. That's the most important quality in a good leader. Don't fall victim to what I call the 'ready, aim-aim-aim-aim syndrome.' You must be willing to fire."[61]

Years ago, I had to make an exceptionally tough decision centered around the standards I needed my staff and leaders to adopt and live out. The guidelines were received well by most; however, there were one or two individuals who struggled with them. They met with me and shared their opinions, but I knew in my heart the decision I had made was the right one. Looking back, I would have made the same decision but with a different approach. Unfortunately, one of the individuals left my leadership and the organization as a whole. I deeply regret this person's decision because I care for them and enjoyed their contribution to the team.

Tough decisions are part of leading and the journey toward Higher Ground. Bill Marriott Sr. expressed his view of decision-making when he said, "Men grow making decisions and assuming the responsibilities for them."[62] Be willing to admit when you are wrong, but never lack the courage to make the tough decision.

David Mahoney admitted that his greatest mistakes stemmed from the decisions he neglected to make. In 1966, he was the head of Canada Dry. The stock was selling at a low price of $11 per share and with about 2.5 million shares outstanding, he could have bought the entire company for $30 million. About twenty years later, he would have been worth about $700 million. A person seeking Higher Ground must make the following decisions:

» Financial
» Personal
» Staffing
» Vision
» Mission
» Hiring
» Firing
» Risk-taking
... and the list goes on.

Others will quickly mark you as a leader or follower, depending on the courage you show to make the tough call; it will make you a doer and set you apart from the dreamers, from a mountain observer to a mountain climber.

COURAGE TO LIVE BY YOUR VALUES

What are values? Values are the set of standards and guidelines that shape your life. It sets in motion your character, your beliefs, and what you will and will not do. Values are a compass that dictates how we live and function in our personal and business lives. For anyone truly committed to excellence and living to their fullest potential, values must be stated and placed firmly into the fiber of your personal and business life.

As I began my journey of building a church from scratch, I had to know our "core values." Once we established them, they became a guide for us. Even now, everything we do is based on these values. If a project does not add to our existing values, we don't do it, even if the project is a great one. My life seems to get busier and busier with each passing day. As a founder of a church, public speaker, author, husband, father, and grandfather, my schedule seems to fill up quickly. However, I have a set of values that guide my schedule. As I am presented with various opportunities and projects, I have to ask myself, *Will this fulfill my values?* For instance, I was recently asked to speak at a camp for teenagers. I value my time, so I had to check my availability in light of my other responsibilities. I value my church and my speaking organization so I have to ask, *Will it fulfill my values? Will it add to my goals?* Ultimately, I had to turn the invitation down. I didn't turn it down because it wasn't a valuable event—I said "no" simply because it did not add to my value or purpose for my life at that time.

You see, that's the value of values—they guide your life and help you make decisions.

You may remember the Tylenol scare that happened in the eighties. Some of the bottles had been tampered with, and they were unsure of how many bottles were affected or the specific cause of the poisonings. The CEO of the Tylenol Company made an executive decision. They pulled all the Tylenol bottles from the shelves across America. It was a record multimillion-dollar loss.

In an interview, the CEO was asked, "How could you make such a quick decision?"

"It was easy," he said, "all we had to do was look at our core values—they made the decision for me."

Your values may differ from someone else's. Let me share a few that I hold close to my heart and serve as a guide for my life:

- » **GOD:** I value my relationship with the Lord. I do not want to do anything or be a part of anything that will negatively affect my personal relationship with Him.
- » **FAMILY:** My family is important to me. I value my wife, my children and their spouses, and my grandchildren, and I do not allow anyone or anything to tear me away from my relationship and time with them.
- » **CHURCH:** The church I started is very important to me. I do not allow projects or events to take away my time or my focus on building this great church.
- » **TIME:** I try to guard my time carefully. I do not like to waste time.

> **HARD WORK:** I value hard work. I believe that you get out of life what you put into it. Work hard, and you will be dealt a good hand in life.
> **LEARNING:** I am a learner. Reading books, listening to tapes, and attending conferences are all part of my routine. I value the learning process.
> **LEADERSHIP:** It is very important to me to develop as a leader and develop leaders around me. I believe the greatness of any organization falls on the shoulders of its leaders.

This isn't an exhaustive list, but they are the compass for my life, guiding me toward what I want to accomplish and what I want to become. It takes "courage" to lay out your values but even more courage to live by them. If you are truly in search of Higher Ground, you will need values. You will need the courage to create them and live by them.

James Patterson and Peter Kim conducted a study of a large representative sample of Americans and asked them, "What would you do for ten million dollars?" One out of four respondents would abandon their families, 23 percent said they would become a prostitute for a week, 16 percent noted they would leave their spouse, and 3 percent confided they would put their children up for adoption. It is one thing to say something is important in your life. It is an entirely different thing to live by it.[63]

As I stated earlier in this chapter, this country was founded on courage, and courage is what makes this country great. Inventors and dreamers have the courage to stick it out. Entrepreneurs are individuals who find courage in the face of uncertainty. Courage is the reason why a couple celebrates its golden anniversary, why a student finishes college, and why small business owners become successful. Whatever your personal Higher Ground may be, decide not to live without courage. Find the courage to keep climbing when you can't see the road in front of you. Find the courage to make the tough decisions that are inevitably coming your way. Find the time to create your own list of personal values and, most importantly, the courage to live them out. Let courage be your ally as you face each day on the mountain.

CHAPTER 10

YOUR FINAL CLIMBING INSTRUCTIONS

I hope you have enjoyed reading this book as much as I have enjoyed writing it. If you have gotten this far, you are in the top 15 percent of America. Approximately 85 percent of people who purchase self-help books never finish them. You are in a class by yourself, and you are on your way to Higher Ground. Whatever your dreams and goals are, you are more than capable of achieving them. You have what it takes!

A while back, I took my entire staff to Six Flags Magic Mountain in Southern California. It was a great day—extremely hot—but still a great day! We enjoyed laughing with one another, kidding around with each other, and bonding as fellow staff members. If you're a leader, never underestimate the advantages of spending time away from the office with your staff. Our day at Magic Mountain was filled with rides, jokes, and plenty of food.

One ride was called the "Dive Devil." It was in the park, but you had to pay for it separately. Anywhere between one to three people strapped on a vest, lay down flat on the ground, and were hooked to a cable attached to an apparatus fifteen stories in the air. Once you were hooked onto the cable, you were then lifted in the air to the top. When you pulled the handle, you were released and would swing down fifteen stories and back up the other side in a sort of half-circle shape. It was like being on a playground swing but fifteen stories high in a Superman position. It was scary, but lots of fun!

I rode it with two of my staff members, Marv and Sonya. Marv was pretty relaxed, I was a little intense, and Sonya was completely nervous. What made us most nervous was probably how quickly they gave us instructions. Within two minutes, they strapped us in the vest and instructed us on what to do and what not to do, even as we were lifted into the air. We had a great time, but delayed instructions made us nervous. I learned something that day—proper instructions help to alleviate anxiety. The more you know, the better you are equipped to face the challenge. That's what I want to do for you in this chapter—to give you some final instructions as you face your personal Higher Ground experience!

You will face challenges regardless of the mountain you climb. Anyone who has done something significant in life or dreamed big has had their share of challenges. The challenges may vary in size, shape, and appearance, but the root of these challenges is typically the same. Let me give you some final facts and instructions to always remember as you face your personal Higher Ground.

LIFE LESSONS FOR ALL HIGHER GROUND SEEKERS

The climb isn't always perfect.

No road worth climbing is perfect. No worthwhile task is ever easy. If it were easy, everyone would be doing it. Marriage is a great experience, but it has its challenges. There's nothing like the love of a child, but parenting is difficult. Receiving a degree in front of a crowd is wonderful, but it takes hard work and facing a variety of challenges to achieve it. The freedom that comes from owning your own successful business is terrific, but not without its share of problems. Any Higher Ground goal will have its share of problems.

I have been privileged to be a part of wonderful projects in my life. Some have failed and some have succeeded, but not a single one of them has been problem-free. The climb has never been perfect for me or for anyone I know. Many individuals start with good intentions to reach their goals but give up too quickly. That's what it takes to achieve your desires. You must be willing to work hard and stick it out. It is not necessarily your talent or ability that gets you to the top; it is a tenacious spirit that never gives up. I have found that people tend to give up early in the climb for one of two reasons.

FEAR

I have talked about this before, but it bears repeating that fear keeps us from climbing—fear of the unknown, fear of failure, fear of what others may say or think, and/or fear of not having enough talent, ability, or education. Fear attacks our minds, grips our hearts, and chokes out our potential. Fear is a funny thing—it makes us afraid of something that has not happened or been proven true. It's like a child who is afraid of the dark.

When my daughter was a toddler, she didn't want me to shut the lights off. I sat down beside her and said, "Close your eyes." She closed them tightly, and then I asked, "What do you see?"

"Nothing," she would say.

Then I said, "Open your eyes." As she opened them, I would ask her, "Now, how can you be afraid of nothing?"

Even though it's a logical argument, it didn't work, unfortunately. The light stayed on. As adults, we fear what we cannot see or predict, and we allow this fear to control us like helpless children. The next time you are overcome by fear, take authority and tell it to go back to where it came from.

IT IS NOT NECESSARILY YOUR TALENT OR ABILITY THAT GETS YOU TO THE TOP; IT IS A TENACIOUS SPIRIT THAT NEVER GIVES UP.

FAILURE

Another reason people give up on the climb to the top is failure. Something didn't go right, or a plan fell through, and rather than pick themselves up and continue the climb, they throw in the towel and let failure get the best of them. Charles Goodyear purchased an Indian rubber life preserver out of curiosity. He began to experiment with the idea of making a weatherproof type of rubber. It was a known fact that the rubber would become hard as stone in the cold weather or melt in the hot weather.

Mr. Goodyear sank all his money into experimenting with this rubber. He worked on this project for five years. In fact, his family sacrificed its standard of living because of Mr. Goodyear's obsession with his experiment. Finally, after thousands of dollars and countless hours, his experiment worked. He figured out a way to make a weatherproof rubber. Out of humiliation, hardship, and defeat, Charles Goodyear won. He turned failure into success and defeat into victory, all because he wouldn't allow failure to be the final answer in his life.

YOUR CLIMBING COMPANIONS MAY LET YOU DOWN

There is nothing like the joy of climbing with other people on your way to the top. I have dedicated an entire chapter to this concept, and I have dedicated my life to helping others succeed and journey alongside me as climbing companions. There is such joy in journeying with others and experiencing the ups and downs of life with people who share your common purpose. Over the years, I have been honored to partner with incredible people. I have brought out the best in them, and they have brought out the best in me. I love working with my staff, being their friends, partnering with them in purpose, and being each other's greatest fans. However, the reality is that, along the way, people will hurt you. There are people that you will pour your life into, and they will, in the end, bring pain to your heart.

People will inevitably let you down as you journey to the top of your Higher Ground. Sometimes, it is possible to repair the relationship through forgiveness and accepting each other's differences, and you can continue climbing side by side. In some situations, you will find the person can no longer be your climbing companion. Although forgiveness is a path you must take to continue the climb, it simply is no longer possible to climb with them.

PEOPLE WILL LET YOU DOWN, BUT NEVER STOP BELIEVING IN THEM, AND DON'T FOOL YOURSELVES—A JOURNEY TRAVELED ALONE WILL NOT BE BETTER.

Before you begin your journey to the top, you must determine to never allow your faith in the human spirit to be shaken, even when disappointment is inevitable. You cannot become isolated because partnership and sharing the experience with others are the greatest sources of joy you will experience throughout your journey! Just because people let you down doesn't mean you should do everything on your own; you will limit your effectiveness if you do that. You cannot accomplish more work with fewer people, or you will rob yourself of the joy that's found in helping others succeed. Finally, you will be tempted to doubt others, and distrust will entice you when they will let you down. Remain hypervigilant of that temptation—don't take the bait. If you do, your relationships with other climbing companions will always be limited because the shadow of doubt in the human spirit will linger in your heart. People will let you down, but never stop believing in them, and don't fool yourselves—a journey traveled alone will *not* be better. Take others with you, and soar your way to the top.

ENJOY THE SCENERY

During a time in my life when I was so focused on tomorrow and couldn't enjoy the present, my good friend Wes Beavis once said to me, "Chris, remember that the path you are on is a marathon, not a sprint; it is a journey, not a destination."[64] I must admit that I fall into this trap quite often. I will find myself so focused on the future, and as soon as the future becomes the present, I focus on the future again. It is a trap that robs me of my joy. Those closest to me must constantly remind me to keep reaching forward in the race while still enjoying the journey.

NO ONE ON THEIR DEATHBED WISHES THEY HAD SPENT MORE TIME AT THE OFFICE.

Remember—although we want to reach our goals, see our dreams become reality, and be known as a Higher Ground climber, we must never become so busy with our futures that we forget the present. Marriages need to be nurtured, and children desperately need our attention. Friendships need to be cultivated, love needs to grow, and joy needs to blossom.

Our Creator did not make us to be so overburdened by life that it robs us of the joy of living.

I am thankful for my wife and two children and their families, who have a perfect way of lifting me to Higher Ground while helping me keep my feet on solid ground. My wife wants me to succeed but never allows me to forget what really matters in life. She helps me remember what I always say to others, "No one on their deathbed wishes they had spent more time at the office." Let me encourage you to keep reaching for Higher Ground but never forget to water your own ground—the ground you call home, family, and friends. Water them with your love and affection, and your journey to the top will never lack the joy your life was meant to have.

IF YOU KEEP CLIMBING, EVENTUALLY YOU'LL MAKE IT

Life has a way of clearing a path for the Higher Ground seeker. For those who want to be more, do more, see more, and become more, life holds a special door open that leads them to the top. Every person who has accomplished something great or has seen their dreams lived out has faced challenges, but they have also found the timeless truth that, eventually, you'll make it to the top—if you keep climbing.

IF YOU DON'T PUT ONE FOOT IN FRONT OF THE OTHER, IT'S A GUARANTEE THAT YOU WON'T GET ANYWHERE.

Throughout the course of my life, I have seen this truth lived out in me. I have watched paths open up before my own eyes

Higher Ground Becomes Shaky Ground Without the Balance of Solid Ground **139**

when I have been determined to reach Higher Ground. However, the key is in the phrase "keep climbing." It's the ability to move forward and upward and never ever stop reaching. There is an old Christmas cartoon where the characters sing a song that says, "Put one foot in front of the other, and, soon, you'll be walking out that door."[65] You can tailor the words to reflect your climbing journey—"If I put one foot in front of the other, eventually I'll make it to the top." You might be thinking, "I have been putting one foot in front of the other, and I haven't made any progress." Consider this: if you don't put one foot in front of the other, it's a guarantee that you won't get anywhere. If you're a Higher Ground seeker, your only choice is to march forward and upward . . . so keep marching!

As I have shared throughout this book, I have been a pastor for a long time. When we were building, we had our share of ups and downs, but we continued to climb toward our Higher Ground. We have found, as we continue to climb, the path to the top has a way of opening up. We purchased the 6.2 acres in June of 2001, and we immediately began the process of working with the city to obtain the necessary permits. We secured an architect, engineer, and project manager, and we were off and running. For anyone who has ever been part of a building project, you know it is a roller coaster ride of emotion. Each day brings a new set of challenges and, quite honestly, it can be very frustrating. Part of the frustration is dealing with the city requirements and codes. There are hoops you need to jump through and red tape that must be crossed.

Throughout the course of the process, we began to feel that our project was not getting the attention it needed. We were in a growing community, and the city had numerous projects to work on—everyone wanted their project done yesterday. In front of our property, there was a street scheduled to meet up with another major street, which would leave our property as the primary corner. This is a great location, but, at the time, it forced us to rely on other people's schedules. Although the new street was a great asset, it had the potential to delay our project in numerous ways.

One day, I was sitting in my office feeling a little frustrated. We found ourselves waiting on other people's schedules, feeling that our project wasn't being prioritized or taken seriously, and unsure of why our questions were not getting answered. It was at that exact moment that I received a phone call from our project manager.

He said, "I've got some interesting news for you." I instantly feared his news would only add to the stress I was already feeling. He said, "Before you bought the property, the original owner had sold approximately two acres to the city, and that left you with 6.2 acres to purchase. The city bought the two acres so that they could bring in the new street. However, the owner of the property and the city itself did not record the grant deed, so in short, you legally own the land that the new street is being built on."

LIFE HAS A WAY OF OPENING UP ROADS TO THOSE WHO SEEK HIGHER GROUND.

As you can imagine, I was astonished, and two words immediately came to my mind: toll road. Obviously, I'm joking (sort of), but this turn of events created quite a stir. That day, we received numerous phone calls from the city and other concerned parties. They wanted us to grant them the two acres that really weren't ours to begin with.

By the end of the day, I found myself reviewing the details of the situation with our project manager and several city officials. I knew the two acres weren't ours, and it wouldn't help us to hold it over their heads because, without their approval, our project would never get completed. However, this turn of events gave us an audience with the city that we desperately needed. During that one-hour meeting, we received in writing that they would finish the street in time and bring in the sewer lines—which had become an issue—and that they would fast-track our project. These questions had been going unanswered, but now, because of this "trump card" we held, our requests were met. From that day, everything moved along, and we received the attention our project needed.

This story represents my earlier sentiment—life has a way of opening up roads to those who seek Higher Ground. I was feeling like a small fish in a big pond, yet a door I could have never opened on my own did. This does not mean it's been easy. This does not mean the road has been a smooth one and that the climb to Higher Ground has been free of obstacles and challenges. I'm simply saying that if you keep reaching for Higher Ground and continue to put one foot in front of the other, eventually you are going to get where you want to go.

ONE FINAL THOUGHT

I said at the beginning of this book that everyone has a Higher Ground—to start a business, write a book, become a noted speaker, own a home, retire early, or learn an instrument or a second language. Everyone has a Higher Ground, a dream they possibly haven't shared with anyone else. My encouragement to you is to use the tools that have been laid out in this book and begin your climb.

Set your course towards the top of the mountain where your dreams have been waiting for you. Brush away the dust of insecurity and fear, and wipe away the filth of a failed past. Determine to view what once seemed impossible with new clarity—recognizing that it is, in fact, possible. It is only then that you will breathe life into your dreams! Destiny awaits you, so embrace it with all your might! Stay focused, march forward, and never settle. Our personal paths may never cross, but if we set our sights on the top, I am confident we will see each other on Higher Ground.

ABOUT THE AUTHOR

CHRIS SONKSEN is the founder of ChurchBOOM, an organization committed to coaching pastors and propelling churches and leaders to reach their potential. ChurchBOOM launched an initiative called Church Rescue which provides coaching, resources, and emergency funding to churches that are struggling and possibly facing closing their doors.

Chris has authored several impactful books for church leaders. Some of his titles include: *When Your Church Feels Stuck, Quit Church, Saving Your Church from Itself,* and *Traction.*

Chris is known for his dynamic speaking and ability to inspire audiences. He is married to his wife, Laura, and has two adult children and two granddaughters.

For more resources go to
www.churchboom.org

ENDNOTES

1   Rev. Todd Bishop, "Remember the Titans: A Call to Do More Than Just Survive," (Bethlehem Assembly of God You Meeting, Valley Stream, NY, March 21, 2001)
2   Dale Gallaway, *Leading with Vision* (Kansas City, MO: Beacon Hill Press, 1999).
3   Gail Matthews, "The Impact of Commitment, Accountability, and Written Goals on Goal Achievement," (podium presentation, 87th Convention of the Western Psychological Association, Vancouver, British Columbia, Canada, May 3-6, 2007).
4   "John Goddard's 'Life List,'" *John Goddard*, https://www.johngoddard.info/life_list.htm.
5   Nelson Algren, *A Walk on the Wild Side* Second Ed. (Farrar, 1998).
6   Dr. Ilene S. Cohen, "Learning to Deal with Your Outer and Inner Critics: A Message for People Pleasers," *Doctor Ilene*, 5 June 2016, https://doctorilene.com/2016/06/learning-to-deal-with-your-outer-and-inner-critics-a-message-for-people-pleasers/.
7   Cynthia Kersey, "7 Big Fat Lies That Critics Will Tell You," *Success*, 16 September 2024, https://www.success.com/7-big-fat-lies-that-critics-will-tell-you/.
8   "The Story of a Man Who Was Fired for a Lack of Creativity but Went on to Build His Own Empire," *Bright Side*, 2023, https://brightside.me/articles/the-story-of-a-man-who-was-fired-for-a-lack-of-creativity-but-went-on-to-build-his-own-empire-798520/.
9   Kersey, "7 Big Fat Lies Critics Will Tell You."
10 Tucker Robbins, "Morning Coffee: SOUND FAMILIAR?" post, *LinkedIn*, 27 Apr. 2015, https://www.linkedin.com/pulse/morning-coffee-sound-familiar-tucker-robbins.
11 *Laverne & Shirley*, Penny Marshall (January 27, 1976; Milwaukee, WI: ABC), Television.
12 David Anspaugh, *Rudy* (October 13, 1993; Culver City: TriStar Pictures).
13 Zig Ziglar, *See You at the Top: 25th Anniversary Edition* (New Orleans, LA: Pelican Publishing, 2000).
14 Max De Pree et al., *Leadership Vol. 5 No. 3*, quoting Christopher Stinnett (Carol Stream, IL: Christianity Today, Inc., 1994), 48.
15 Bill Kynes, "A Hope That Will Not Disappoint." In *Best Sermons No.* , ed. James W. Cox (New York, NY: HarperCollins, 1989).
16 Robert H. Schuller, *Success Is Never Ending, Failure Is Never Final: How to Achieve Lasting Success Even in the Most Difficult Times* (Ealing, London: Bantam, 1990).
17 Nancy Brewka Clark, "Nathaniel Hawthorne's Struggle and Romance with Salem," *Literary Traveler*, 16 July 2006, https://www.literarytraveler.com/articles/hawthorne_salem_ma/.
18 Nathaniel Hawthorne, *The Scarlett Letter, Dover Thrift Editions* (Garden City, NY: Dover Publications, 1994).
19 Jim Collins, *Good to Great: Why Some Companies Make the Leap . . . And Others Don't* (New York, NY: Harper Business, 2001).
20 Charles H. Cooley, "Looking-glass self. The production of reality: Essays readings on social interaction," *Teaching Sociology* 30 (1902).
21 Daniel Ockey, "The Man Who Sold Hot Dogs," *Medium*, 23 Jun 2018, https://medium.com/@danielockey/the-man-who-sold-hot-dogs-3c3f48a49613.
22 Walter Wintle, "Thinking," *Unity College Magazine* (Unity Tract Society, Unity School of Christianity, 1905), lines 1-4, 13-16.
23 Keith Harrell, *Attitude Is Everything: 10 Life-Changing Steps to Turning Attitude into Action* (New York, NY: Collins, 2000).

24   Henry Ford, "Whether you think you can, or think you can't—you're right," quoted in Jim Boomer's *CPA Practice Advisor*, 15 July 2014, https://www.cpapracticeadvisor.com/2014/07/15/whether-you-think-you-can-or-think-you-cant-youre-right/15980/#:~:text=Jim%20Boomer-,A%20famous%20Henry%20Ford%20quote%2C%20"Whether%20you%20think%20you%20can,and%20certainly%20for%20technology%20initiatives.
25   Winston Churchill, speech at the Lord Mayor's banquet (London, November 9, 1954).
26   William Arthur Ward, quoted in Pat Obuchowski, "Positivity Trumps Negativity," wall post, *LinkedIn*, 27 Sept. 2017, https://www.linkedin.com/pulse/positivity-trumps-negativity-master-executive-leadership-coach.
27   Henry Ford, quoted in Joe Griffith, Speaker's Library of Business Stories, Anecdotes, and Humor (Saddle River, NJ: Prentice Hall Direct, 1990), 253.
28   Griffith, *Speaker's Library of Business Stories, Anecdotes, and Humor*
29   Marcel Schwantes, "Science Says 92 Percent of People Don't Achieve Their Goals. Here's How the Other 8 Percent Do," *Inc.*, 26 July 2016, https://www.inc.com/marcel-schwantes/science-says-92-percent-of-people-dont-achieve-goals-heres-how-the-other-8-perce.html.
30   Ramón Menéndez, *Stand and Deliver* (March 11, 1988; Burbank, CA: Warner Bros.).
31   Guest, Allen Edgar. *Don't Quit* (poem).
32   John Mason, *Know Your Limits—Then Ignore Them* (Sevierville, TN: Insight Publishing Group, 1999).
33   Horace Mann, *Thoughts Selected from the Writings of Horace Man* (H.B. Fuller, 1867), 115.
34   Andrew P. Hills et al., "'Small Changes to Diet and Physical Activity Behaviors for Weight Management," *Obesity Facts* 6, no. 3 (2013): 228-238, https://doi.org/10.1159/000345030.
35   James O. Hill et al., "Obesity and the environment: Where do we go from here?" *Science* 299 (2003): 853-855.
36   Susan J. Rodearmel et al., "Small changes in dietary sugar and physical activity as an approach to preventing excessive weight gain: The America on the Move Family Study," *Pediatrics*, 120 (2007): 869-879, https://doi.org/10.1542/peds.2006-2927.
37   Susan J. Rodearmel et al., "A family-based approach to preventing excessive weight gain," *Obesity* 14 (2006): 1392-1401, https://doi.org/10.1038/oby.2006.158.
38   Emerson, Ralph Waldo. *Success* (poem).
39   "Boy Scouts Oath, Motto, and Law," Boy Scouts of America, https://www.scouting.org.
40   Harris Interactive, *Values of Scouts: A Study of Ethics and Character*, Report produced by Boy Scouts of America (Youth and Family Research Center, 2005).
41   Mississippi Valley Council, *Scouting Makes a Difference!* (Boy Scouts of America, 2003).
42   Thomas Jefferson, extract from letter to Peter Carr, August 19, 1785.
43   Teresa Ghilarducci, *Work, Retire, Repeat: The Uncertainty of Retirement in the New Economy* (Chicago, IL: University of Chicago Press, 2024).
44   Lane Gillespie, "Bankrate's 2025 Emergency Savings Report," *Bankrate*, 23 January 2025, https://www.bankrate.com/banking/savings/emergency-savings-report/.
45   "Alina Comoreanu, "Credit Card Statistics," *WalletHub*, 9 January 2025, https://wallethub.com/edu/cc/credit-card-statistics/25581.
46   Matt Schulz, "2025 Credit Card Debt Statistics," *LendingTree*, 8 January 2025, https://www.lendingtree.com/credit-cards/study/credit-card-debt-statistics/.

47   Yvonne Charlotte Anne-Marie de Gaulle, "The presidency is temporary—but the family is permanent," quoted in David Young, *Breakthrough Power for Leaders: A Guide to an Extraordinary Life* (Wind Runner Press, 2012).
48   Emma Goldman, *Anarchism and Other Essays* (Overland Park, KS: Digireads.com Publishing, 2019).
49   Max Lucado, *A Love Worth Giving: Living in the Overflow of God's Love* (Nashville, TN: W. Publishing Group, 2006).
50   J.P. Vaswani, *Burn Anger Before It Burns You* (Wisdom Tree Publishers, 2015).
51   Ron Underwood, *City Slickers* (June 7, 1991; Culver City, CA: Columbia Pictures).
52   Martin E. Seligman and Peter Schulman, "Explanatory Style as a Predictor of Productivity and Quitting Among Life Insurance Sales Agents," *Journal of Personality and Social Psychology* 50, no. 4 (1986): 832-838, https://ppc.sas.upenn.edu/sites/default/files/predictproductivity.pdf.
53   Ann Reed Wilder et al., "The Relationship Prayer Has on Quality of Life in Later Adulthood," *Proceedings of the ASSR* (2016): 109-199, https://www.researchgate.net/profile/Ann-Wilder/publication/303722323_The_Relationship_Prayer_has_on_Quality_of_Life_in_Later_Adulthood/links/574f8d1308aebb988044f68c/The-Relationship-Prayer-has-on-Quality-of-Life-in-Later-Adulthood.pdf.
54   Cristina Sanda Emrich, "Spouses' Scriptural Beliefs, the Faithfulness of Relationship with God, and Marital Satisfaction," PhD diss., (Liberty University, 2022).
55   "Facts About Divorce In American 2024," *Terry & Roberts*, 6 May 2024, https://terryandrobertslaw.com/blog/divorce-rate-facts/.
56   Axel Neree, "Couples that pray together, stay together," *Medium*, 25 November 2019, https://medium.com/@axelneree/couples-that-pray-together-stay-together-5afac89cd439#:~:text=Statistic%20say%20that%20~50%25%20of,church%20together%20end%20in%20divorce.
57   Thomas G. Plante et al., "The Association Between Strength of Religious Faith and Psychological Functioning," *Pastoral Psychology* 48, no. 5 (2000): 405-412, https://doi.org/10.1177/003463738908600204.
58   Zig Ziglar, "What Money Won't Buy," Filmed January 5, 2012, *YouTube*, https://www.youtube.com/watch?v=8w0Ahfj1jCw.
59   Mark Twain and R.D. Gooder, *Pudd'nhead Wilson and Other Tales* (Oxford, England: Oxford University Press, 1894).
60   President Dwight D. Eisenhower, "No matter what the weather looks like, we have to go ahead now. Waiting any longer could be even more dangerous. So let's move it!" quoted in Joel A. Garfinkle, "What's the Perfect Job for Me?", *Dream Job Coaching*, https://dreamjobcoaching.com/resources/articles/whats-the-perfect-job-for-me.
61   Pickens, T. Boone. Commencement speech, George Washington University, 1988.
62   Bill Marriott Sr., "Men grow making decisions and assuming the responsibilities for them," *Gettheedge*, 15 October 2015, https://www.gettheedgeuk.co.uk/the-marriott-management-philosophy/.
63   James Patterson and Peter Kim, *The Day America Told the Truth: What People Really Believe About Everything That Really Matters* (Upper Saddle River, NJ: Prentice Hall Direct, 1991).
64   In a conversation with Wes Beavis.
65   Jules Bass, *Santa Claus Is Coming to Town* (December 13, 1970; Burbank: ABC).

www.ingramcontent.com/pod-product-compliance
Lightning Source LLC
Chambersburg PA
CBHW050911160426
43194CB00011B/2358